Quiz
Book on Islam

For All Levels of Expertise

Husain A. Nuri

Weekend **Learning**

To contact the publisher, e-mail at weekendlearning@gmail.com

Copyright © 2007 by Weekend Learning Publishers.

First edition February 2007

ISBN 0-9791916-0-2
ISBN 978-0-9791916-0-2

Library of Congress Control Number: 2006940841

Weekend Learning Publishers
http://www.WeekendLearning.com

Printed in India

رَبِّ اَوْزِعْنِيٓ اَنْ اَشْكُرَ نِعْمَتَكَ الَّتِيٓ اَنْعَمْتَ عَلَىَّ وَعَلٰى وَالِدَيَّ وَاَنْ اَعْمَلَ صَالِحًا تَرْضٰهُ وَاَدْخِلْنِيْ بِرَحْمَتِكَ فِيْ عِبَادِكَ الصّٰلِحِيْنَ ۞

"My Rabb! permit me to give thanks for Your blessing which You have bestowed upon me and upon my parents, and that I may do good which pleases You, and admit me, with Your mercy, among Your righteous bondsmen." (27:19)

I dedicate this small effort to my parents.

Table of Content

Preface

The idea of this book was conceived in the year 2000 when Principal of Dayton Islamic School Part Time Program, Sr. Ruqayyah Islam, requested me if I would be interested to conduct an inter-school Islamic quiz competition to be hosted by the school. I volunteered to be the Quiz Master with great degree of interest, mainly to rake my knowledge base and to make the competition a fun filled learning environment. Soon I had more challenges in my hand than I had expected. I was not sure how easy the questions should be or how deep should I probe? Not knowing much about depth of knowledge of the students in typical weekend schools in the US, I thought of challenging them with interestingly worded questions, with some twists in them. I selected few questions that I thought were 'easy' and few that I thought were 'difficult.' My idea was to challenge the students, but to my amazement they challenged me with the depth of knowledge that I did not expect them to demonstrate.

With six weekend schools from Cincinnati, Columbus, Dayton, Indianapolis and Toledo, the first Annual Quiz Bowl competition was a great success. The parents, teachers, students, audience and judges were thrilled. So was I. The bar was raised for me as well as for the contestants for the years to come. I thoroughly enjoyed being the Quiz Master for the next six years. Each year the contestants, principals and parents asked me – which book to use to prepare for the competition and how to prepare. Since there is not a single book that I could refer, obviously the challenge for the contestants and Quiz Master became difficult. There is no short cut to win the competition. One has to increase the knowledge base to win. In each of the past six years, the teams that won the competition had one or more star performers whose knowledge base was deep and broad. However, I truly felt a quiz book could help many parents and students prepare for the competition. At least the book might serve as necessary vehicle to guide them in the right direction, but may not serve as a 'formula' for sure success. With this viewpoint in mind, I prepared this book.

This book has over fourteen hundred questions, with few repeat questions in various formats under various categories. The idea is to present the same question from different angle and perspective. To the best of my knowledge and ability I have verified the answers and attest to their accuracy. The principals and teachers from many schools also reviewed the book. Nevertheless the burden of any omission or error is entirely mine. I sincerely acknowledge the help, suggestions, comments and encouragements received from Sr. Ruqayya Islam, Dayton; Dr. Mohammed Salikuddin, Cincinnati, Dr. Ghulam Saklayeen, Dayton, Alauddin Alauddin, Columbus during various phases of this work. I am also grateful to audience, contestants, parents and teachers who provided valuable suggestions about the questions I had asked in the competition.

Behind every work, big or small, there are always visible and invisible inspirations. I am grateful to Allāh for providing me with inspirations, knowledge and ability to finish the book. Throughout the course of the work my wife Shamim Nuri encouraged me—I sincerely appreciate her support. I am also indebted to my brother Dr. Mansur Ahmad for helping me with the layout of the book, cover design and various other technical suggestions. My two sons Arif and Imran helped me during various stages of competition, starting from just being there with me to prepare the PowerPoint presentation, printing the manuscript and even shredding the volumes of pages after I edited them. They often regretted since I would not allow them to participate in the competition I conducted simply to maintain fairness and neutrality of the competition. I will consider myself successful if students and parents find this book of some value during practice session or simply to enhance knowledge.

Columbus, OH   Husain A. Nuri
February 2007

beginnersQuiz

The Prophet, His Family, His Life - I

1. How old was Muhammad (pbuh) when he received the first revelation?

2. For how many years the revelation continued to reach the Prophet?

3. What is the term that denotes the way of life of the Prophet?

4. She was the wife of the Prophet when he received the first revelation. Who was she?

5. She was the daughter of Wahb Ibn 'Abdi Manāf and the mother of Muhammad (pbuh). Who was she?

6. What is the name of the cave in which the Prophet received the first revelation?

7. What was the general profession of Muhammad (pbuh) when he was a young man?

8. At what age did Prophet Muhammad (pbuh) pass away?

9. This person was the guardian of young Muhammad (pbuh) after his parents passed away. Who was he?

10. This close family member was the first woman to embrace Islam. Who was the person?

11. The tribe of the Prophet was the Quraish, what was the name of his clan?

12. Before any daughter was born to the Prophet, a son was born to him. What was this son's name?

13. The Prophet had four daughters; all of them grew up and got married. Who were they?

14. She was the most beloved wife of the Prophet, she is also credited as narrator of thousands of ahadīth. Who was she?

15. The Prophet's most beloved daughter Fātimah was married to this person. Who was he?

16. After the young Muhammad's (pbuh) first guardian died, this person became his guardian.

17. What was the first major battle fought by the Prophet Muhammad (pbuh)?

 Answers on page 92

The Prophet, His Family, His Life - II

1. The Prophet's great great grandfather was this person. Who was he?

2. During the childhood Muhammad (pbuh) visited Syria with this uncle. Who was he?

3. In the year 575 C.E., six years after Muhammad's (pbuh) birth, this person passed away.

4. In the year 570 C.E., a s troop of elephants attacked Makkah. Another landmark event happened the same year. What was that event?

5. The youngest son of 'Abd al-Muttalib was related to the Prophet in certain way. What was that relation?

6. How many children did the Prophet and his first wife Khadījah had in total?

7. Only this child of the Prophet outlived the Prophet (was alive when the Prophet passed away). Who was the child?

8. Among all his uncles, one was very hostile to Muhammad (pbuh). Who was that uncle?

9. What important event happened on 12th Rabi al-Awwal on 11 A.H?

10. The Quraish gave this favorite nickname to Muhammad (pbuh) before he became a prophet of Allah. What was that nickname?

11. At the invitation of Aws and Khazraj, the Prophet Muhammad (pbuh) did something significant in the year 622 C.E. What was that?

12. When did Muhammad say 'wrap me up, wrap me up'?

13. After receiving the revelation, how long was the Prophet married to Khadījah before she passed away?

14. The Prophet and Abū Bakr hid in this cave when they fled form Makkah. What was the name of the cave?

15. This term denotes the event when the Prophet traveled from Makkah to Jerusalem.

16. This nursing mother suckled infant Muhammad (pbuh) for two years. What was her name?

2

Answers on page 92

Names of Allāh

1. A qualifying name of Allāh meaning 'the Beneficent'.

2. A qualifying name of Allāh meaning 'the Most Merciful' or 'the most Gracious'.

3. A qualifying name of Allāh meaning 'the King' or 'the Sovereign Lord'.

4. A qualifying name of Allāh meaning 'the Creator'.

5. A qualifying name of Allāh meaning 'the Generous One'.

6. A qualifying name of Allāh meaning 'the Forgiver'.

7. A qualifying name of Allāh meaning 'the Noble' or 'the Glorious'.

8. A qualifying name of Allāh meaning 'the Light'.

9. The meaning of Allāh's qualifying name Al-Hamīd.

10. The meaning of Allāh's qualifying name As-Sabūr.

11. The meaning of Allāh's qualifying name Al-Wāhid.

12. The meaning of Allāh's qualifying name Al-Hakīm.

13. The meaning of Allāh's qualifying name Al-'Adl.

14. The meaning of Allāh's qualifying name As-Salām.

15. The meaning of Allāh's qualifying name Al-Alīm.

16. The meaning of Allāh's qualifying name Al-Hafīz.

Terminology -I

1. The general term of the prayer call given out loudly by a person.

2. This term denotes the written accounts of the doings or sayings of the prophet.

3. A term in Islamic law that describes something as forbidden. What is that term?

4. This term denotes something which is disliked and is wrong in Islam. What is that term?

5. This term stands for people praying Salat behind the Imam. What is the term?

6. The curved place in the front wall of the Masjid denoting the direction of the Qiblah, used by the Imam to lead the prayer. What is that place called?

7. This lesser pilgrimage can be performed any time of the year when one visits the Ka'bah.

8. Any of the early Muslims who migrated to Madīnah in the lifetime of the Prophet. What is the general term to denote these Muslims?

9. The direction towards which the Muslims face during their daily prayers.

10. This term stands for the act of going around the Ka'bah seven times.

11. This term denotes one unit of salāt. What is the term?

12. The Qur'ān uses this term to describe the Hypocrites. What is the term?

13. This term denotes a way of remembrance of Allah, especially by chanting His names in a Sufi way of devotion.

14. This term denotes a formal legal opinion given by a scholar or jurist on the matter of a particular Islamic law. What is the term?

15. This term stands for college of Muslim higher education. What is the term?

16. This term denotes seclusion in the Masjid during the last ten days of Ramadan for the purpose of worshipping Allah. What is the term?

17. What is the Arabic word used to mean commentary of the Qur'ān?

Answers on page 93

Terminology -II

1. This Arabic term denotes life after death. The term also includes the Day of Judgment and the life to follow.

2. This term denotes the Madīnan Muslims who helped the Prophet and the immigrants from Makkah.

3. When a Muslim dies, people pray a special salāh for the deceased person. What is that salāh called?

4. This term denotes compulsory duty, prescribed by Allāh. What is the term?

5. When a person performs salātul Witr, a special du'ā is recited. What is the name of the du'ā?

6. During the month of Ramadan, Muslims take a pre-dawn meal. What is the term used for this meal?

7. This term denotes voluntary charitable contribution made by a Muslim.

8. This term means guardian. But this term is used to denote one who memorized the Qur'ān, as if he is the guardian of the Qur'ān. What is the term?

9. During wudū, water is to be used. But Islam also allows for dry wudū or dry ablution. What is the term used for this act?

10. What is the month immediately preceding the month of Ramadān in Islamic calendar?

11. The Qur'ān uses this term to mean angel Jibrīl, but the term is also used to mean soul of a person. What is the term?

12. What is the Arabic term that stands for marriage between a man and a woman?

13. What is the term used to identify a person who is qualified to issue Fatwā?

14. This term denotes the tax levied upon non-Muslim citizens in an Islamic state. What is the term?

15. This term denotes the science of determining Islamic law and jurisprudence. What is the term?

16. This term denotes the tenth day of the first Islamic month, Muharrahm. What is the term?

Past Prophets -I

1. Allah appointed this brother of Mūsā to assist him in his mission to Egypt. Who was he?

2. Two prophets had to do something about ships; one was Nūh, who was the other?

3. He was nephew of Ibrāhīm, also a prophet. Who was he?

4. He was the last of the Jewish prophets. Who was he?

5. He was the most majestic and richest prophet of all time. Who was he?

6. This prophet had used iron for the first time for his armory. Who was he?

7. This prophet had appointed a camel as a sign for his community. Who was the prophet?

8. Among the father-son prophets mentioned in the Qur'ān, they were the last. Who were they?

9. Mūsā and Hārūn were two brother-prophets. There is another instance in the Qur'ān where two brothers were prophets. Who were they?

10. This prophet made best use of various technologies, such as navigation in sea etc. Who was he?

11. This prophet is most frequently mentioned in the Qur'ān. Who is that prophet?

12. When Sulaimān was inspecting the troops, this bird was missing. What was that bird?

13. In how many tribes the Children of Israel were divided at the time of Mūsā?

14. Sara was one of the wives of the prophet Ibrāhīm, who was the other?

15. Which prophet's community was destroyed as their men wanted to marry other men?

16. When this prophet was a young boy, he was sold as a slave by some traders. Who was he?

17. The angels advised this prophet to walk away by night and not to look back, but his wife looked back. Who was that prophet?

Past Prophets -II

1. This prophet was known to have skills to interpret dreams. Who was the Prophet?

2. People rescued an infant from a basket afloat a river. Later the infant grew up to be a prophet. Who was the prophet?

3. Shaitān told this prophet if he ate from an object he would become immortal. Who was the prophet?

4. This young prophet broke some idols to teach the people that idol worshipping is useless. Who was the prophet?

5. Before becoming a prophet, this person accidentally killed an Egyptian. Who was this would-be prophet?

6. The prophet investigated if the sun, the moon or the stars could be gods of people. Who was the prophet?

7. People refused to talk to this prophet since they believed he was child in the cradle. Who was the prophet?

8. This prophet prayed for three days and three nights before he was convinced a son would be born to him. Who was the prophet?

9. Allāh named this son of a prophet. Later, the son would also become a prophet. Who was he?

10. This prophet was one of the poorest prophets, it is said no body was as poor as this prophet. Who was he?

11. This prophet told his people not to harm a camel, but the people did not listen. Who was their prophet?

12. This prophet chained the shaitān, made the jinns work for him and extract pearls from sea. Who was the prophet?

13. This prophet was wealthy, healthy and had many sons, but gradually he lost his wealth and health, and his children died. He became sick. Who was the prophet?

14. This prophet was not very eloquent, so he wanted his brother to assist him in his mission. Who was the prophet?

15. This prophet became disgusted with his people, so he abandoned the community and boarded a loaded ship. Who was he?

 Answers on page 94

The Qur'ān

1. What was the month in which first few verses of the Qur'ān was revealed?

2. What is the total number of sūrahs in the Qur'ān?

3. The entire Qur'ān can be divided into various parts, called Juz. How many Juz are there in the Qur'ān?

4. What is the literal meaning of the word "Qur'ān"?

5. How many years did it take for the Qur'ān to be completely revealed?

6. Who was responsible to deliver the Qur'ān to the Prophet?

7. What is the name of the cave where the first set of verses of the Qur'ān was revealed?

8. How many verses were revealed to initiate the revelation of the Qur'ān?

9. The sūrahs of the Qur'ān were revealed in two cities, one was Makkah, what was the other?

10. The first set of verses contain name of a tool normally found on a desk or a table. What is that?

11. The very first revealed verse of the Qur'ān instructs people to do something. What was the instruction?

12. What is the name of the longest sūrah in the Qur'ān?

13. This term means commentary and explanations of the Qur'ān.

14. This person ordered and made sure that the Qur'ān was compiled and bound into one volume. Who was the person?

15. What is common among Yusuf Ali, Muhammad Asad, and Pickthall?

16. For ease of reading the Qur'ān can be divided into seven parts. This term stands for every seventh part of the Qur'ān.

17. What is the name of one of the best known scribes of the Qur'ān at the time of the Prophet?

18. An angel was engaged to bring the revelation of the Qur'ān to the Prophet. Who was the angel?

Sūrah

1. A sūrah in the Qur'ān is named after a large war animal. What is the title of the sūrah?

2. How many Ayahs are there in the shortest sūrahs (there are 3 such sūrahs).

3. This sūrah tells about the Majestic night – the night when Qur'ān was revealed.

4. This term denotes various smaller sections of any sūrah.

5. Only one sūrah in the Qur'ān is named after one of the Prophet's uncles. What is that sūrah?

6. This sūrah contains the seven oft-repeated verses. What is that sūrah?

7. This sūrah talks about whispering of jinns. What is that sūrah?

8. Unity and Oneness of Allah is declared in this sūrah.

9. Only sūrah in the Qur'ān named after a woman. What is that sūrah?

10. Two sūrahs in the Qur'ān bear names of arthropods. One is 'Ankabūt, what is the other?

11. Only sūrah that does not start with "*Bismillāh*." What is the sūrah?

12. How many times does "*Bismillāhi ar-Rahmāni ar-Rahīm*" appear in the Qur'ān?

13. Sūrah at-Taubah is also known by another name. What is that name?

14. In this sūrah, the story of Dhul-Qurnain is related. What is the name of the sūrah?

15. Which small sūrah talks about earthquake and proceeding to the Judgment?

16. The opening verse of the sūrah Baqarah bears three letter abbreviations. What are the abbreviations?

17. Which sūrah is symbolically termed as *sab al-mathānī*?

18. Which sūrah is symbolically termed as mother of the Qur'ān (*umm al-kitāb*)?

Personality

1. This was the Christian name of Muhammad Ali, the legendary heavy weight boxer, before he converted to Islam.

2. What was the name of the Prophet's paternal grandfather.

3. Of the four caliphs, this person served for the longest period of time. Who was he?

4. What was the name of Fir'awn's (Pharaoh) wife, who was a righteous woman.

5. This legendary person traveled with Mūsā during his quest for knowledge.

6. He was the founder of modern secular Turkey. Who was he?

7. Who was the author of the famous book 'The Bible, the Qur'ān and Science'?

8. When she was elected the Prime Minister of Pakistan in 1988, she became the first woman to head a government of an Islamic State. Who was she?

9. This great Muslim military leader was called "Sword of Allah." What is his name?

10. By this name the famous Muslim physician Ibn Sina is known to the west.

11. This Jewish convert is known to have narrated largest number of ahadīth.

12. This Saudi king was assassinated in the year 1975. Who was he?

13. This famous Mughal emperor is known for his tolerant policy towards Hindu population. What was his name?

14. A medieval most famous Mongol military genius, sources of many legends. What is his name?

15. Famous Muslim basketball player who represented the Los Angeles Lakers during 1975-89. What was his name?

16. In the heavyweight boxing sports (until 2005), two Muslims were World Heavyweight Boxing champion; one was Muhammad Ali, who was the other?

17. He was a famous Persian poet, known for composing monumental book titled Shāhnāma.

First

1. He was the first Mu'adhdhin ever appointed to pronounce Adhān, who was he?

2. What was the first battle in which the Muslims defeated a vast army of the Quraish?

3. The first mosque built by the Holy Prophet was at this place.

4. The first five verses of the Qur'ān was revealed on this night of Ramadan. Which night was it?

5. He was the first youth to embrace Islam. What is his name?

6. The first person to become the Khalīfa after the death of the Prophet.

7. What was the name of the first child born to the Prophet?

8. What was the name of the first daughter born to the Prophet and Khadījah?

9. The first five verses revealed are part of this sūrah.

10. What was the destination of the first Muslim migration to a foreign country?

11. Who was the first Khalīfa to conquer Al-Quds/Jerusalem?

12. On this day, the first official day of Hajj is commemorated.

13. This person committed the first crime of homicide in the history of human civilization.

14. This person was the first Muslim in to go to the space aboard a spaceship.

15. The first Muslim to win Nobel Prize in any discipline.

16. After receiving the revelation, the prophet undertook first significant trip outside of Makkah to this place.

17. She is the first Muslim woman to win Nobel Peace prize. What is her name?

18. Of the three Jewish tribes in Madīnah, this tribe was the first expelled due to their hostility towards the Muslims. Who were they?

"M-" Word

All answers to begin with the letter "M-"

1. What is the term for a designated person who gives the prayer calls?

2. Jesus was often addressed by this symbolic name. What is that?

3. The tower in a mosque from which prayer calls are given out.

4. Shī'ite Muslims believe this person will appear on the earth during the last days of the world.

5. One of the two angels in Babylon, blamed to have taught magic to the people.

6. What is the Arabic term for the dower money paid to wife, without which marriage would not be legal?

7. The niche in the wall of any mosque indicating the direction of Qiblah.

8. What is the name of the school of law founded by Ibn Anas?

9. She was mentioned as the daughter of 'Imrān, and was also mentioned as sister of Hārūn. Who was she?

10. Quails and this "M-" thing were sent to the Israelites as good food during the time of Mūsā.

11. What is the name of an angel, who is often regarded as 'guardian angel'?

12. What is the Arabic term for one who has performed hijrah and settles in a new place?

13. What is the term used to denote the Prophet's mystic journey to the Heaven?

14. This is said to split up as an indication of the Hour drawing near.

15. Shu'aib preached to the people of Ashab al-Aika who are also known as the people of this place. What is the place?

16. A person who outwardly believes in Islam but in his heart he denies faith. What term is used to denote such a person?

17. What is the name of the place where Mūsā lived for about eight years, a place where prophet Shu'aib also lived.

 Answers on page 95

"S-" Word

All answers to begin with the letter "S-"

1. What is the Arabic term for the Companions of the Prophet?

2. What is the name of the hillock near Ka'bah from where the pilgrims make the first walk to the hillock of Marwāh?

3. During the prayer you must go this position when you say '*subhāna rabbiyal a'la*'.

4. A term used to denote a person who has sacrificed his life for Allāh's sake.

5. Muslims don't do this, but the polytheists are routinely doing this with Allāh.

6. What is the term for the biography of the Prophet as well as his Companions?

7. What was the name of the country that was ruled by Queen Bilqīs?

8. What is the term used in the Qur'ān for the Jewish sacred day of a week?

9. What was the name of the prophet sent to the people of Thamud?

10. One of the cities of prophet Lūt, destroyed for the transgression of its people.

11. One of the four Imams who founded a school of thoughts for the Sunni Muslims.

12. What is the name of the fountain in Paradise, mentioned in the Qur'ān?

13. This term is used to denote written books of Ibrāhīm or Mūsā. Sometimes it is also used to mean small pamphlets of the Qur'ān.

14. What is the term for the law based on the Qur'ān and Traditions of the Prophet?

15. After you end this month, next month would be the month of fasting.

16. The Prophet gave a special title to Khālid Ibn Walīd, the famous commander of the Muslim army. What was the title in Arabic?

17. The Qur'ān says this person was responsible in misguiding the Israelites after they were rescued by Mūsā?

18. They don't believe in Khalīfas, instead believe in the Imams. They believe there were twelve Imams. Who are they?

Fathers, Grandfathers

1. He was the father of Muhammad (pbuh), whom the prophet never saw.

2. He was 'Ā'isha's father, who was a prominent Companion of Muhammad (pbuh).

3. He was Hafsah's father, who was a prominent Companion of Muhammad (pbuh).

4. He was father of Yūsuf, who was also a prophet. Who was he?

5. He was father of Yahyā, who himself was a prophet. Who was he?

6. He was father of Sulaimān, a great warrior prophet. Who was he?

7. He was the father of Ismā'īl. Who was he?

8. Father of Ibrāhīm was a polytheist. Who was he?

9. He was the father of Ruqayyah, Qasim and Ibrāhīm.

10. He was the father of Hamzah, Abū Lahab, Abu Tālib, Az-Zubayr.

11. 'Ali was son of Abū Tālib. Who was 'Ali's grandfather?

12. The early Muslims quickly named this audacious man of Makhzum as 'father of ignorance'.

13. The first Umayyad caliph's father was a notorious enemy of the Prophet, but he accepted Islam after the fall of Makkah.

14. Ja'far and his wife were one of the few early converts to Islam, but his father was not a Muslim. Who was the father?

15. This woman was affectionately called the "mother of her father." Who was she?

16. His name meant 'father of the kittens.' He was a Jewish convert, famous for narrating Hadīth.

Miscellaneous – I

1. The pilgrimage to Makkah to perform Hajj must be done in this month. What is the month?

2. What is the first month of the Muslim calendar?

3. What is the last month of the Muslim calendar?

4. This famous uncle of the Prophet died in the battle of Uhud. Who was he?

5. What is the name of the 30th part of the Qur'ān?

6. This prophet rebuilt the Ka'bah. What is his name?

7. One of the two main rivers of Iraq is Tigris, what is the other one?

8. This term identifies the followers of Islam, but it is also the name of a collector of Hadīth.

9. Through this angel Allāh revealed the Qur'ān to the Prophet. What is his name?

10. This person was lying asleep in the bed of the Prophet Muhammad (pbuh) to fool the assassins on the night of the Prophet's Hijrah to Madīnah.

11. In the story of Yūsuf, he saw a dream when he was a child. What was that dream about?

12. In the modern world, this country has the largest population of Muslim.

13. The term for the medieval study of chemistry aimed at converting base metals into gold.

14. During the early days of Islam, the Muslims faced this place during their prayers. What was the place?

15. What is the term for sacrifice offered by the parents of a newborn child, particularly to name the child?

16. What is the original name of Makkah as mentioned in the Qur'ān?

17. A woman from Banu Sa'd was the wet nurse for infant Muhammad (pbuh). What was her name?

18. He was an Ethiopian born Muslim, a Companion of the Prophet. Due to his beautiful voice, the Prophet asked him to give Adhan.

Miscellaneous – II

1. When Muhammad (pbuh) married Khadījah, she was 40 years old. How old was Muhammad (pbuh) at the time of marriage?

2. At what age did the Prophet pass away?

3. What was the original name of Madīnah?

4. Only city in the world where people could be facing east, west, north or south during their salat.

5. This tribe signed the Treaty of Hudaibiyah with the Muslims.

6. The Arabic term for 'a sign' also the meaning for 'a miracle' and 'a verse.'

7. Who paid the money to free Bilāl from slavery?

8. The last Muslim empire that lasted all the way into the 20th century. What was its name?

9. Only two of the Prophet's wives bore him sons, one was Khadījah, who was the other?

10. Before the advent of Islam, Ka'bah was protected from the army of this invader. What was the name of the invader?

11. This person was the Prophet's cousin, later he became his son-in-law. Who was he?

12. The place where the Tawrat was revealed to Mūsā. What was the place?

13. He is the compiler of the most authentic book of Hadīth. What is his name?

14. This prophet was willing to sacrifice his son after he had a dream. Who was he?

15. The term in Arabic collectively refers to the Jews and the Christians as the People of the Book.

16. What two groups of people did Dhul Qurnain imprison to protect the mountain people?

17. What was the first Muslim dynasty formed soon after the rule of Four Rightly Guided Khalīfa ended?

Miscellaneous – III

1. What is common with Dā'ūd, Nasā'ī, Musilm and Tirmidhī?

2. During the last years of the Prophet, when he was very sick, who did he ask to lead the prayers even though he was present in the congregation?

3. What is known by the term *Hajjatul Wida*?

4. What did the Prophet say symbolically lie at the feet of a person's mother?

5. Which small sūrah says large crowds would join Islam?

6. One of the Khalīfas ruled for only two years three months and ten days. Who was he?

7. Angel Jibril always brought revelations to the Prophet. But only once he asked him to "read." When was it?

8. When a person performs obligatory Jummua prayer, how many times he would have said '*rabbana lakal hamd*?'

9. How many verses does the most frequently recited sūrah contain?

10. The Qur'ān says sawm is prescribed to you as it was prescribed to others. What is meant by the word sawm?

11. Who did the Prophet mainly engage to write down the revelations during the Prophet's lifetime?

12. In which English calendar year (in C.E.) did the Prophet pass away?

13. Abū Bakr emphasized collecting the chapters of the Qur'ān into a book format. Who ultimately completed the compilation?

14. What role did Anthony Quinn play in the famous biographical movie "Muhammad"?

15. *Rub al-Khali* (lit. Empty Quarters) is a vast barren desert in this country. What is the country?

16. Who is popularly called as Ata Turk or The Father of the Turks?

17. He was a Persian scholar, author of about 450 books on a wide range of subject. His books on medicine were used as text book in European universities for seven centuries. Who was he?

advanced**Quiz**

"A" Word

The answers should begin with the letter "A-"

1. When this event will happen, the world will be turned into a new world.

2. Jaf'ar, a cousin of the Prophet was a member of delegation to this country.

3. He and his army had to perish due to a pestilence in 570 C.E. What was his name?

4. When this sets in, men will be at loss except four types of people.

5. Vast empty land, thus the name of the place where pilgrims assemble.

6. On 10th of Muharram the tragedy of Karbala is commemorated. What it is called?

7. This gulf flanks the Sinai Peninsula in its eastern border.

8. The five pillars of Islam is also known by this word.

9. The 99-names of Allah are the "Most Beautiful Names". What are these called in Arabic?

10. The last Muslim presence in Spain was in Granada, where a famous mosque known by this name still exists.

11. He is one of the six compilers of Hadīth.

12. Name of a sūrah in Juz 30, the title signifies swift horses.

13. Some commentators think Dhūl Qurnain was this great person. Who was . he?

14. Reported in a Hadīth, she is one of the four 'perfect women.' Who is she?

15. Name of 29th sūrah that makes a passing reference of an insect. What is that sūrah?

16. A title of a sūrah in Juz 30, meaning congealed blood.

17. What is the title of the 100th sūrah that speaks about galloping swift horses?

18. Who first prayed to Allāh saying: Our Rabb! We have done wrong to ourselves, and if you do not forgive us and have mercy on us, we shall surely become the losers.

"B" Word

The answers should begin with the letter "B-"

1. The two angels Hārūt and Mārūt belonged to this city.

2. Expedition to Tabuk was undertaken to counter a possible attack by this empire.

3. In 18:31; 22:23; 35:33 the Qur'ān says righteous people will wear _____ in the Paradise.

4. The Qur'ān says he was imprisoned in Egypt for a crime not committed by him. Who was he?

5. In sūrah Taubah, Allah said the worst people in hypocrisy are these people. Who were they?

6. Title of sūrah #98 – it talks about manifest proof. What is the title?

7. The African slave of Umayyah, tortured for believing in One God. What was his name?

8. This creature is sometimes used in the Qur'ān to mean bad luck or ill omen.

9. A term for an animal whose ear is slit and let loose by the Pagan Arabs in honor of some idols.

10. The intermediate state for the soul after the death of the body, before they are raised up.

11. Arabic term indicating a child has reached the age of legal maturity.

12. This 'house' is reportedly in the seventh heaven, visited by the Prophet during his night journey.

13. This term signifies an innovation in the name of religion.

14. What is the short title of well known collection of Hadīth?

15. A term used in theology to mean something that is hidden in meaning.

16. Muslims believe a missing Gospel of this person existed but it is not compiled in the present day Bible. Who was the author of the gospel?

17. This term denotes public money of a Muslim state that the ruler cannot use for his personal expenses, but only for the public good.

"C" Words

The answers should begin with the letter "C-"

1. Dhu al-Qarnain used this metal to seal the gaps in the walls.

2. The very last wife of the Prophet was originally follower of a Christian Church of this denomination.

3. Mūsā wanted to have his people settle in this land. What was the land?

4. This battle titled in the name of an animal, was fougth between 'Alī and 'Ā'ishah.

5. The largest Muslim civil liberties group in America working to enhance Islamic understanding and empower American Muslims.

6. Series of campaign by West European armies to capture Holy Land from the Muslims.

7. The old name of the largest city north of Turkey, where Europe and Asia meets, was the center of many Roman and Muslim conquests.

8. One of the famous frameworks to end Arab Israel conflict, brokered by President Carter, President Sadat and Prime Minister Begin. What was the name of the accord?

9. According to the Bible, the Qur'ān and the Hadith, nobody will enter the Paradise until _____ enters through the eye of a needle.

10. A specific shape of the moon, it symbolizes Islam.

11. Islam advocates freedom of religion, therefore in the matter of faith one cannot do this to others.

12. In the story of seven sleepers, they were asleep in this place.

13. English word for a type of forbidden food mentioned in the Qur'ān.

14. What is the English term for a woman slave, usually captured in war? The Qur'ān talks a great deal about their rights.

15. In Sūrah Mā'idah verse 82, the Qur'ān praises certain type of Christian religious persons, identified as *qissisīn*. What is the English term for these people?

16. In sūrah An'ām they are termed as gifts of Allāh, for man ride on them or eat them.

"D" Words

The answers should begin with the letter "D-"

1. This Arabic term is equivalent to Antichrist. It is used about an imposter who would appear during the last days of the earth and create disorder.

2. This city was conquered by Khālid Ibn Walīd during the rule of Khalīfa 'Umar. The city is known as a holy city in Islam.

3. What was the name of the Prophet's mule or horse that was part of many legends?

4. The prophet, who not only first used iron, but also possessed skill with birds and animal. Who was he?

5. On the Day of Judgment a person will be judged based on the level of good or bad of this thing.

6. This term is used for silver coins. Yūsuf was sold for a number of these coins.

7. A small distinct religious community in Lebanon, whose faith is Islam but strongly influenced by Greek philosophy and other religion.

8. In Arabic it is termed *qard* or *qarz*. What English term is used to this term?

9. What would happen when the heavens would cleave asunder and the stars would disperse and the seas would be made to flow and the graves would be laid open?

10. When you convey the message of Islam to others, essentially you have done this activity.

11. The Heaven is mentioned as an abode of peace in the Qur'ān. What is the term for abode of peace?

12. This Persian word is used for a person who lives by begging but otherwise he is a spiritual person.

13. What is the English term used to describe the enormity of punishment suffered by the people of Nūh?

14. He is the Shaitān, the evil. In English usage he is often mentioned with this term.

15. During marriage a husband is obligated by law to give this to his wife as a mark of respect. What is he required to give?

"G" Word

The answers should begin with the letter "G-"

1. Hoarding of this item so as not spend in the path of Allāh is highly condemned in the Qur'ān.

2. One of the two great sins that appear to have some benefit in them, but the sin is greater than the benefit.

3. What is the term for frequent raids undertaken in pre-Islamic periods to obtain booty?

4. A sūrah titled 'The Overwhelming Event' talks about the events during the Day of Awakening.

5. The Qur'ān says certain drinks in the Heaven will have the flavor of this root spice. What is that?

6. The word means an under-aged boy, but it also means slave.

7. King Tālūt killed this evil monster. What was his name in English?

8. One of the twin cities destroyed by Allāh for their wicked practices.

9. Indulgence in this conduct without correct knowledge is strictly forbidden in Islam.

10. What is the general term for the New Testament books narrated by Mark, Matthew, Luke and John?

11. A term denotes something that cannot be seen, or that cannot be explained, or something secret.

12. This Arab tribe often formed allies with the Jewish tribes of Madīna and conspired against the Prophet.

13. The first chapter in the Bible is this one. What is the name of the chapter?

14. The general English term for *Jannat* or Paradise.

15. Hārūn was not responsible, but it was Sāmirī who was the mastermind behind making this thing.

16. A region north of Palestine, much of Jesus's early ministry was confined to that region.

"H-" Word - I

The answers should begin with the letter "H-"

1. Islamic calendar was started to commemorate this great event. What is that event?

2. One of the pillars of Islam, usually related with vast assembly of mankind.

3. Wife of a prophet left infant child alone when she went in search of water. Who was she?

4. This prophet was wrongfully blamed to have made golden calf. Who was he?

5. One of the wives of the Prophet safe kept a complete copy of the Qur'ān. Who was she?

6. The great gathering place – identified with the day of Awakening.

7. Prophet of the 'Ād – in whose name sūrah 11 in the Qur'ān is named. Who was he?

8. A treaty between the Muslims and the Quraish was named after a place located right outside of Makkah.

9. The pilgrims are not required but many of them kiss this stone during Hajj at Ka'bah.

10. What was the name of a large idol in the Ka'bah. Some say it was the largest of all idols.

11. One of the uncles of the Prophet, portrayed in a movie by Anthony Quinn. Who was the uncle?

12. Although not mentioned by name, in the first human crime, this brother was killed by the other wicked brother.

13. The disciples of the prophet 'Isā was mentioned by this term in the Qur'ān.

14. On the day of Awakening, this organ/part of the body will symbolically rise to the throat out of grief.

15. This important court member of Fir'awn acted vehemently against Mūsā and mocked his teachings.

16. He was grabbed by his beard and head for allegedly causing rift among the Israelites.

"H" Word - II

The answers should begin with the letter "H-"

1. This woman of Bani Sa'd enjoyed working as foster mother. She was made famous for nursing a special infant. Who was she?

2. An English term applied to people who believe in Islam but in their heart they are opposed to Islam.

3. This activity is prohibited near the sacred precincts during the pilgrimage.

4. This surah talks about every slanderer, defamer who hoards wealth and counts it.

5. A Palestinian militant group, even won a national election.

6. A title of respect applied to king, prophets, sahabas, saints, etc. to express sacredness of their character.

7. A radical group based in Lebanon, often fight against terrorism or they are blamed as terrorists.

8. A type of Hadīth that are said to be words of Allah, but it is not part of the Qur'ān.

9. This Shi'ah Imam left the world and believed to return on the Day of Judgment. He is Mahdi. What is the other "H-" word we are looking for?

10. A historical region south of Arabia along the gulf of Aden and Yemen, ruled by Queen of Sheba and served by Prophet Hūd.

11. The title of 57th sūrah, in the name of a metal. What is that?

12. A name of Allāh, it means "guardian" or "protector". A person can also have this title if he protects the Qur'ān by becoming one of this.

13. Seven sūrahs in the Qur'ān starting from sūrah 40 through sūrah 46 starts with this abbreviation.

14. This mountain near Makkah is intimately associated with the history of the Prophet. What is it?

15. Sulaimān loved them, so did the Prophet. But Sulaimān summoned them and massaged their legs and necks. Who are we talking about?

16. What is the name of the valley about three miles from Makkah where a battle took place between the Muslims and the Hawāzin?

"K" Word

The answers should begin with the letter "K-"

1. It literally means a cube. Known from the antiquity, this is center of Islamic world.

2. It means 'one who covers.' Usually is used to indicate one who covers the truth.

3. The word means 'great.' Usually associated with 'great sin', and sometimes about 'great idol.'

4. The word means 'the word.' It is a pillar that makes a person Muslim.

5. What is the term used for the shroud used for the dead. Usually it is a white piece of cloth.

6. The word is used only twice in the Qur'ān, in both instances to mean 'soothsayer.' What is the term?

7. A city in 'Irāq, known for famous martyrdom of Husain.

8. What is the name of the robe that covers the Ka'bah?

9. It is the name of an Arabian tribe. It is also the name of a Jewish chief in Khaibar. What is the name of the tribe or the chief?

10. Just as Pharaoh is the name of any king in Egypt, this is the general name of all kings in ancient Persia.

11. A sermon delivered before a particular prayer as well as before two 'Eid prayers.

12. A prior agreement for the purpose of dissolving a marriage at a later time. It is not Talaq. What is the term?

13. Literally means 'the green one.' This person is narrated in a story in sūrah Al-Kahf.

14. The name of a tribe in Madīnah. They were in fight with another tribe. They invited the Prophet to meditate disagreement between two tribes.

15. This term is used to denote a tax payable on the land. 'Umar used this tax on the land he conquered in 'Irāq.

16. A rich and populous valley north of Madīnah, inhabited by the Jews. In the year 7 A.H. the Prophet led an expedition to this place and defeated the Jewish chief Kinānah.

"M" Word

The answers should begin with the letter "M-"

1. She was one of the female goddesses inside the Ka'bah. Who was she?

2. What is the term for a person who narrates Hadīth or one who is learned in the Traditions?

3. If taziyah are brought out by the Shi'ah Muslims, it must be this month.

4. Title of any Muslim warrior who wages jihad.

5. A term usually denotes death; it is always used in the Qur'ān to mean departure of soul from body.

6. A general term standing for relatives with whom marriage is unlawful.

7. Name of the station in Makkah where the pilgrims assume *ihram*.

8. When India was struggling to get its independence, the Muslims were represented by a political party that ensured formation of Pakistan. What was that political party?

9. A Muslim jurist who employs *Ijtihad* can be called as this:

10. This medieval group of thinkers, who used "rational" interpretation of the Qur'ān, often gave very irrational interpretations.

11. This word is sometimes used to denote religion of Ibrāhīm or religion of other prophets.

12. A term used to denote bond-slaves, later the term was used to denote the body of slaves who ruled Egypt for a long time.

13. This term denotes a person who has no property; a poor person.

14. The Qur'ān mentions this past religious group – that if they associate with Allāh, on the Day of Awakening Allāh will decide their affair. Who were they?

15. What is the term for a tooth cleaner, made of a twig of a tree. The Prophet used to clean his teeth with these.

16. What is the name of a small mat, cloth or carpet on which a Muslim prays?

"Q" Word

The answers should begin with the letter "Q-"

1. This wicked brother killed his innocent brother and did not bother to bury him. Who was the wicked brother?

2. One of the sons of the Prophet, died within two years of his birth. Who was he?

3. Jerusalem used to be this for the Muslims until it was changed to Makkah.

4. Muslims built their first mosque at this place. What was the place?

5. Mūsā came with a clear proof to Fir'awn, Hāmān and this person. Who was the person?

6. Name of a sūrah—talks about The Great Calamity.

7. What is the term for a person who recites the Qur'ān correctly and with beautiful tone?

8. A great traveler, monarch nicknamed "Lord of Two Horns", built the great walls. Who was he?

9. A prominent tribe in Arabia. They were caretaker of Ka'bah during the advent of Islam.

10. According to the Qur'ān mountains would crumble due to fear of Allāh if this was sent to them. What is that?

11. The title of sūrah #54, named after one of the visible object in the sky.

12. The name of sūrah #68, a valuable tool in shaping human civilization, also mentioned in the first set of revelation.

13. The unbelievers deny many a thing; among them the agnostics invariably deny this event.

14. The Qur'ān mentions that this tribe was protected during their journey in the winter and the summer. Which tribe was that?

15. The process of analogical reasoning of the learned with regard to the teachings of the Qur'ān.

16. According to the Qur'ān, the Jews and the Christians do not agree upon their own "Q*" and they don't believe in the Muslim's "Q*" either.

"T" Word

The answers should begin with the letter "T-"

1   It is a valley in the northwest of Arabia, scene of an expedition undertaken by the Prophet to thwart possible attack by Roman Empire.

2   What is the general term for the Companions of the Prophet?

3   A small city close to Makkah. Its inhabitant chased away the Prophet and pelted stones at him when he went to preach there. What is that city?

4   A name of Shaitān, but the term also stands for certain idols worshipped by the Quraish.

5   The title of the 20th sūrah. It is reported after 'Umar listened to the parts of this sūrah, he accepted Islam.

6   What is the general term for the expression *Allāhu Akbār*, usually spoken out loud?

7   What is the name of the book that contains traditional laws of the Jews?

8   This independent tribe of Makkan origin, occupied northeastern part of Najd. They fought by the side of the Prophet during the Hunain war.

9   This term stands for any explanation of a book, but usually it is used for the commentary of the Qur'ān.

10 He was a distinguished Companion, son of 'Ubaidaullāh. He is honored as one of the ten people promised to enter Paradise.

11 This term is used to denote blind following of a religious leader without applying proper reasoning.

12 This is a title of a sūrah, but it also means expressing repentance.

13 What is the name of the sacred valley in connection with Mūsā, mentioned in sūrah 20 and 79?

14 What is the general term for reading or reciting of the Qur'ān?

15 This word stands for the name of a fountain mentioned in the Qur'ān. What is the term?

16 A king of Israel, mentioned in the Qur'ān. He fought against Goliath.

Earlier Prophets – I

1. Two other prophets were contemporary to Mūsā, one was his own brother Hārūn, who was the other?

2. A draw of lots was used to determine fate of this prophet. Who was the prophet?

3. This prophet could interpret dreams. Who was he?

4. Mūsā received his revelation at this Mountain. What was that mountain?

5. This prophet traveled with Khidir in search of knowledge.

6. Brothers conspired to kill him but later dropped him in a well. Who was this person, who later became a prophet?

7. Opinion differs, but he can be considered to be the only Ethiopian prophet named in the Qur'ān. Who was he?

8. The tribe of Thamūd lived in a place north of present day Arabia. What was the place?

9. This prophet served notorious twin cities where people were lewd and immoral. Who was the prophet?

10. Son of this prophet thought he could save himself, but Allāh did not save him because he was a sinner. Which prophet's son are we talking about?

11. Of all things, this prophet made a camel as a sign for Thamūd. Who was the prophet?

12. People of this prophet curved out dwellings on the rock. They lived in the lower peninsula in the ancient Arabia. Who was the prophet?

13. The Qur'ān indicates no prophet was ever slain; however, the Bible says this Baptist was beheaded. Who was he?

14. If Mūsā would marry this person's daughter, Mūsā would get shelter for 8-10 years. Who was this person?

15. The story of this prophet largely deals with advice to his son and best conduct with parents.

16. This prophet is credited to have used iron for the first time. Who was the prophet?

Earlier Prophets – II

1. This prophet employed people to dive into the sea to extract pearls. Who was the prophet?

2. In the story of Yūsuf, the king dreamed of certain animals eating other animals. What were the animals?

3. He was the only prophet who admitted he had some speech impairment. Who was the prophet?

4. Allāh destroyed a community with fierce wind blowing over them for seven nights and eight days. Who were these transgressing people?

5. This prophet first gave himself the title "Muslim" and chose it for his descendants and followers.

6. What two groups of people did Dhu-l Qurnain imprison to protect the mountain people? Who were the people?

7. When Mūsā was traveling with his young servant, what thing did the servant forget?

8. What is the reason Mūsā fled from Egypt when he was a youth?

9. When the ten half-brothers made up a story that an animal devoured Yūsuf, which animal did they mention?

10. During his journey Mūsā said he would go on for ages but would stop if he reached this. What did he mention that would end his journey?

11. One prophet specifically told his people not to cheat or short measure goods in scale. Who was the prophet?

12. Disbelievers directly blamed this prophet for practicing witchcraft. Who was the prophet?

13. On seeing or sensing fire burning in the hill, this prophet approached it and received revelation.

14. This prophet passed a judgment on litigation about a pack of sheep belonging to one person destroyed crop field of another person. Later his judgment was changed. But who was the prophet?

15. As a proof of power of God, which prophet placed birds in four hills and called them to him. Who was the prophet?

16. Due to a famous incident, this prophet is also known as Dhu an-Nūn.

Former Prophets - Trivia

1. During one of the expeditions, this prophet smiled at the response given by the opponent and prayed to Allāh for kingdom. Who was the Prophet?

2. This prophet gave a judgment involving two brothers who were disputing about 100 ewes. Who was the prophet?

3. A prophet in the Qur'ān was likened with prophet Ādam. Who was that prophet?

4. Ifrit, a stalwart was engaged to do some job. Under which prophet did he work?

5. One of the verses in the Qur'ān asks a past prophet to hold some twigs in hand and beat his wife with it. Which prophet was so instructed?

6. When this past prophet was busy with some work, people used to pass by and laugh at his work. Who are we talking about?

7. This past prophet wanted the horses brought back to him and then he massaged their body. Who was the prophet?

8. This past prophet came out of his place of worship and silently instructed his followers to devote day and night in worship. Who was he?

9. This prophet told his father to do what he was instructed to do, and he would willingly comply. Who was the prophet?

10. The father of this prophet was angry with him and said he would drive him away. In response the prophet said he would ask Allāh to forgive him. Who was the prophet?

11. The Qur'ān says this past prophet was innocent, kind hearted and never rude to his parents. Who was he?

12. The Qur'ān says this prophet's mother moved to an eastern place where the prophet was born. Who was the prophet?

13. This past prophet prayed to Allāh to have an inheritor who would inherit the teachings of Yaqub. Who was the prophet?

14. After this prophet was born, his mother was divinely instructed to eat, drink and cheer her eyes. Who was the prophet?

15. He was tired, fatigued. He sat down under a tree and prayed to Allāh saying he was needy for whatever good He might send towards him. Which prophet are we talking about?

Prophet Muhammad (pbuh) - I

1. What was the clan to which the Prophet Muhammad (pbuh) belonged?

2. The prophet passed away in this year. What year was it under Islamic calendar?

3. Due to this nickname earned by Muhammad (pbuh), the rich merchant lady Khadījah entrusted him with the responsibility of trading her merchandise.

4. For how many years the Prophet was married to Khadījah?

5. According to the Qur'ān, Jesus foretold the advent of Muhammad (pbuh). He used a name for him. What was the name?

6. Before reaching the age of 40 years, which prophet's religion Muhammad (pbuh) was following?

7. Due to certain events, the tenth year of the Prophet's mission is commonly called as what?

8. On seeing a child Muhammad (pbuh), this monk prophesized that when he grew up he would be a prophet.

9. The Prophet made his last pilgrimage of Ka'bah and delivered his sermon at Uranah Valley of Mount Arafat on the 10th Hijrah. How many Muslims were present at the valley?

10. This important event, mentioned in the Qur'ān in sūrah Banī Isrā'īl took place in Makkah one year before Hijrah.

11. Of the ten sons of 'Abd Al-Muttalib, the youngest one was special in some way. What is that?

12. This daughter of Khuwaylid is related to the Prophet in certain way. What is that?

13. The Prophet had two wives by the name of Zainab. One of them was Zainab bint Jahsh. What was the identifying name of the other Zainab?

14. She was the eldest daughter of the Prophet and Khadījah. Who was she?

15. The Prophet had a son born to him from his Egyptian Coptic wife Māriyah. What was his name?

16. This Christian reassured Muhammad (pbuh) after the first revelation that he indeed was a Prophet of Allāh.

Prophet Muhammad (pbuh) – II

1. Who was the blind man from whom the Prophet turned away his attention?

2. In this sūrah, the Prophet was disapproved for turning away from a blind man.

3. Altogether, how many wives did the Prophet have in his life?

4. The Prophet undertook an expedition against Roman Emperor Heraclius. Which sūrah deals extensively about this expedition?

5. Revelation of this complete sūrah indicated that the Prophet might pass away soon afterwards.

6. After paying 40 ounces of gold and planting 300 date palms, this person was freed and became a famous Companion of the Prophet. Who was he?

7. After Khadījah died, the Prophet married a widow, who would take care of his children. Who was she?

8. What was the relationship between Ruqayyah, Al-Qāsim and Al-Tāhir.

9. Who was the very last woman to be included as wife of the Prophet?

10. In a famous battle, the Prophet fell down and was almost killed. He lost one of his teeth. What was that battle?

11. The Prophet used to like this product, but in order to make him dislike the product, some of his wives told him when he ate it his mouth had bad breath. What was the product?

12. The disbelievers in Makkah used to blame the Prophet were a *Kāhin*. What did they mean?

13. Madīnah is located north of Makkah, but during his migration to Madīnah, the Prophet fled in a different direction. What was that direction?

14. The Prophet married daughters of two of the future Caliphs. One was Abū Bakr's daughter. Name the other Caliph and his daughter.

15. During the battle of Khandaq, the Prophet used a unique battle strategy. What was the strategy?

16. The Prophet had a long discussion with famous Christian delegates who came to question him about Jesus and other aspects of Islam. From which place did these delegates come?

Al-Qur'ān

1. What is the total number of verses in the Qur'ān?

2. How many sūrahs in the Qur'ān begin with the abbreviation *alif-lām-mīm*?

3. What is commonly known as *al-Shifa, al-Haq, al-Hakim, al-Nūr, al-Rahmah*?

4. Mahmood Khalil al-Hussary, Saad Al-Ghamdi and Abd al-Basit are famous for this work on the Qur'ān.

5. The first revelation of the Qur'ān started in this night of the month of Ramadan, agreed by most scholars.

6. How many alphabets are used in forming the *muqatta'āt* or abbreviated letters in the beginning of various sūrahs?

7. How many sūrahs start with abbreviated letters called *muqatta'āt*?

8. What is the only sūrah to start with two sets of abbreviated letters in its first two verses?

9. Under whose supervision the first authorized copy of the Qur'ān were compiled, copied and circulated?

10. Technically the only difference in the text between the earliest copies Qur'ān compiled under supervision of 'Uthmān and the later days Qur'ān. What is the difference?

11. Where in the Qur'ān the famous *Ayat al-Kursi* is found?

12. This sūrah is symbolically called as the 'Heart of the Qur'ān.'

13. One symbolic name of the Qur'ān is *Al-Furqān*, which other divine scripture is also called *al-Furqān*?

14. This person was the most renowned scribe of the Qur'ān. Who was he?

15. Unbelievers wanted Qur'ān to be reveled to a prominent man of Makkah or this city.

16. A symbolic prostration or sajdah is recommended after reading certain number of verses of the Qur'ān. How many such verses are in the Qur'ān?

Al-Qur'ān - Trivia

1. What is the total number of ruku in the Qur'ān?

2. How many sūrahs were revealed in Makkah?

3. How many Madīnan sūrahs are in the Qur'ān?

4. What Arabic letter sign is used by the side of the Qur'ān to indicate it is a rukū'?

5. Where in the Qur'ān the Prophet was named as Ahmad?

6. In which category of creature does the Qur'ān classify Iblīs into?

7. In which book of the non-Muslims the term Qur'ān is repeated many times?

8. In which year the vowel marks or Tashkeel were added in the Qur'ān?

9. The Qur'ān classifies its verses under two broad categories based on the meaning they convey. What are the two categories?

10. In exact year, month and days, how long did it take to reveal the Qur'ān?

11. What is the term for the interval between the first and second set of revelations?

12. How many different names of Allāh are mentioned in the Qur'ān?

13. Who is the only non-prophet person named in sūrah Yūsuf?

14. The Qur'ān states someone is *Khataman Nabiyyen*. Who was he?

15. Who first restricted the recitation of the Qur'ān be done in the style of the Quraish?

16. Which is the first prostration verse in the Qur'ān?

17. Where in the Qur'ān Allāh instructed people to say *sallāhu 'alaihi wassalam* after saying the Prophet's name?

18. In which sūrah in the Qur'ān first detailed dietary laws for Muslims can be found?

Battle

1. In this battle, prophet was greatly injured and rumor spread that he died.

2. In this battle 313 Muslims fought against the Quraish. What was the battle?

3. Archers left their position in this battle causing heavy loss to the Muslim army. Which battle was that?

4. During this battle the Quraish occupied higher parts of the hill whereas the Muslims were subjected to the lower reaches of the hill.

5. Before the battle started, rainfall strengthened Muslim position. What was that battle?

6. Half-hearted Muslims found various excuses not to participate in many battle preparations. But they strongly opposed during this preparation.

7. Initial plan to ambush a caravan soon led to this battle. What was that battle?

8. According to the Qur'ān 1,000 angels helped the Muslim army in this battle.

9. According to the Qur'ān 3,000 angels helped the Muslim army in this battle.

10. Soon after the return from Hūdaibiyya, in this battle Muslims achieved a near victory.

11. In this battle 3 miles east of Makkah, the Muslims suffered heavy initial damage when Hawazin archers suddenly ambushed them.

12. 5,000 angels helped the Muslim army in this battle, but the battle was not fought face to face. Which battle was that?

13. The valley between Makkah and Tā'if, where the Prophet defeated the pagans. What was the battle?

14. Salmān al-Fārsi suggested an innovative way of warfare that gave the Prophet clear victory in a battle. What was the innovative way?

15. This man, nicknamed by the Muslims as "the father of ignorance", was the most prominent adversary to be killed in the battle of Badr.

16. According to the Qur'ān what percent of the spoils of war is prescribed for the state?

Companions

1. This person lied down on the bed in disguise while Muhammad (pbuh) fled from his house.

2. The cousin and ward of the Prophet was the first youth to converts to Islam. Who was he?

3. This Companion is credited to have given first Adhān in Madīnah.

4. This Khalīfah, whose Caliphate lasted 12 years in turmoil, ended with his assassination.

5. This famous Companion was son of Abū Tālib. He fell bravely at the battle of Mu'tah.

6. A Persian slave Fīroz assassinated this Khalīfah. Who was the Khalīfah?

7. In the battle of Uhud when many archers left their position to obtain the loot, their team leader stayed in his position. Who was he?

8. This person, son Abū Sufyān, succeeded as ruler of Islamic world after the 4th Khalīfah.

9. This Caliph was assassinated near Kufa and with him ended the reign of rightly guided Khalīfahs.

10. He was the Prophet's freedman and adopted son. Who was he?

11. What title did the Prophet give to 'Umar ?

12. This Companion often gave classes on interpretation of the Qur'ān and in course of time was recognized as the first exegete of the Qur'ān.

13. The Prophet's daughter Ruqayyah was married to this Companion, but after she died, the Prophet's another daughter Umm Kulthūm was married to the same Companion. Who was he?

14. This person fought against the Prophet in the battle of Uhud, later accepted Islam and became one of most successful general in expansion of Islamic dominion. Who was he?

15. This son-in-law of the Prophet later became the ruler of Muslim world, and his murder would lead to the first fitnah.

16. This Iranian Christian traveled long distances, was held as slave, later accepted Islam when he was emancipated by Muhammad (pbuh) and became an esteemed Companion.

The Hereafter

(Note: While describing various features of the Hereafter, the Qur'ān uses parables and semantics in earthly terms).

1. Many Ahādīth narrate the hell would have certain numbers of doors. How many are generally mentioned?

2. In the hell the face and outfit of the dwellers would be smeared with this item.

3. Snake like fruits in the Hell would originate from a tree. What is the name of the tree?

4. Whips in the Hell are made up of this metallic substance.

5. The Heaven will contain a type of tropical fruit of the genus *Musa*.

6. The garment in the Heaven will be of this type of costly fabric.

7. Other then the rhizome flavored drink, another flavor of drink in the Heaven would be this. Name the flavor.

8. The available fragrances in the Heaven would have this aroma.

9. A fountain by this name would be available in the Heaven.

10. This word indicates the standard greetings in the Heaven.

11. One who is in authority or the angel appointed to preside over the Hell.

12. On the day of Awakening, the disbelievers will be given books of deeds on their left hand and to their one side. What is that side?

13. During the Hereafter youths would pass around drinks to everybody. These youths are stated to be pure and compared with a precious item. What is the item?

14. In the heaven this valuable gift of mollusk origin will be given as gift.

15. The Qur'ān indicates all people, including prophets, would be interrogated during the Day of Judgment. Which prophet would be interrogated the most?

16. The dwellers of the Heaven would be welcomed with a greeting of 'Salām' and someting would be spread out for them. What is that?

Sūrah – I

1. What is the general term for various abbreviations, e.g. *Alif Lām Mīm* in the beginning of a sūrah?

2. In terms of number of verses, these 3 sūrahs are the smallest in the Quran. What are they, and which is the smallest?

3. A dog is mentioned in a story in the Qur'ān. What is that sūrah?

4. Defeat of the Romans and their subsequent victory is mentioned in this sūrah.

5. Sūrah # 10 derives its title from solitary mention of a prophet and fish.

6. Which sūrah contains the passage: "this day I last perfected for you your religion and completed upon you my blessings and accepted for you Islam as the religion."

7. Only sūrah that does not start with "*Bismillāhir rahmānir Rahīm.*"

8. The only sūrah where the incident of Mi'rāj is mentioned.

9. What sūrah bears the theme of whispering into the heart by the jinns and mankind?

10. What sūrah bears the theme of wife becoming carrier of fire wood to burn them?

11. What sūrah bear the theme of one who drives away orphans, does not feed the poor and unmindful of salāt?

12. What sūrah makes it clear that men are at loss except people doing four types of deeds?

13. What sūrah talks about the majesty of the night—peace until the rising of the sun.

14. What sūrah talks about fig, olive and Mount Sinai?

15. What sūrah deals with the theme of when the earth quakes, people will see atom's weight of good or evil?

16. What sūrah foretells about a great calamity when mankind will be like moth scattered.

Answers on page 105

Sūrah – II

1. What sūrah talks about multiplication divert you but then you will visit graves … you will soon know.

2. What sūrah touches upon the theme of a plot turned into confusion and birds casting baked clay?

3. The title of the 103rd sūrah, also means time through ages, or part of the day.

4. What is the only sūrah in the Qur'ān named after a plant?

5. Two sūrahs in the Qur'ān are named after metals. What are they?

6. Two sūrahs bear a title consisting of a single letter. What are the titles?

7. A common item on your desk is also the name of a sūrah. What is the item?

8. The only sūrah to bear the name of a community outside of Arabia.

9. One sūrah in the Qur'ān bear the name of a very large animal. What is that sūrah?

10. Which sūrah mentions the punishment of 100 stripes for adultery?

11. Certain numbers of sūrahs begin with two letter abbreviations *Hā Mīm*. How many such sūrahs are in the Qur'ān?

12. Three sūrahs talk about *ribā*. Two of them are Baqarah and Al-e-'Imrān. What is the third sūrah?

13. Kneeling down and prostration are two positions showing utmost humility. Which sūrah bears a title indicating kneeling down?

14. Kneeling down and prostration are two positions showing utmost humility. Which sūrah bears a title indicating prostration?

15. Various sūrah deal with the timing of a day. What is the most common sūrah to bear a title indicating the time when daybreaks?

16. How many verses does the longest sūrah in the Qur'ān have?

17. The Qur'ān prescribes fasting in the month of Ramadan. But in two different verses, Allāh allows sick and travelers to fast on other days. In which sūrah the permission is given?

 Answers on page 105

First Verse of a Sūrah

1. Which sūrah starts with: Say, O you Unbelievers!

2. Which sūrah starts with: Have you seen him who belies religion?

3. Which sūrah starts with: Surely We revealed it in the night of majesty?

4. Which sūrah starts with: He frowned and turned aside?

5. Which sūrah starts with: Consider the Fig and the Olive?

6. Which sūrah starts with: Glorify the name of the Rabb, the most High?

7. Which sūrah starts with: Consider the Heaven full of constellation?

8. Which sūrah starts with: They ask you about voluntary gift. Say voluntary gift belong to Allāh and the Rasūl...?

9. Which sūrah starts with: O you, the one wrapped up!

10. Which sūrah starts with: An immunity from Allāh and His Rasūl in respect of those polytheists with whom you made a covenant

11. Which sūrah starts with: Glory be Him Who transported His bondsmen by night...

12. Which sūrah starts with: The Hour draws near and the moon splits up.

13. Which sūrah starts with: Allāh has already heard the sayings of her who pleads with you...

14. Which sūrah starts with: Surely We sent Nūh to his people, saying; "warn your people..."

15. Which sūrah starts with: Say: "It has been revealed to me that a party of the jinn listended..."

16. Which sūrah starts with: *Kāf, Hā, Yā, 'Ayn, Sād?*

17. The second verse of the sūrah says: This book, there is no doubt in it, a Guidance for those who fear God. What is the first verse of this sūrah?

18. The translation of the second verse of the sūrah is: Did He not turn their plot in confusion? What is the first verse of this sūrah in Arabic?

Answers on page 105

"Ibn - "

1. Great philosopher and specialist in medical sciences, whose works are still taught in many universities.

2. This Ibn Abdullāh is regarded as one of the greatest reformers in the history of mankind.

3. He is one of the six principal compilers of Hadīth. Who is he?

4. A famous Moroccan traveler who traveled about 75,000 miles and covered almost all the medieval Muslim countries.

5. This 14th century Syrian theologian whose 14-volume work is often regarded one of the foremost classical commentaries of the Qur'ān.

6. This student of Imam Shāfi'ī—a leading figure of the ahl al-Hadīth, founded a school of law named after him.

7. This second son "Ibn 'Ali Ibn Abū Tālib" is more popularly known by this name.

8. This cousin of the Prophet, regarded as the first interpreter of the Qur'ān, often gave critical interpretation of the Qur'ān.

9. He was the first of the Umayyad Caliphs. He was Ibn Abū Sufyān, but what was his actual name?

10. He lived mostly in Madīnah. He was the founder of the one of the four school of Islamic jurisprudence. Who was he?

11. A great navigator of the 15th century, who guided Vasco da Gama's fleet from Africa to India.

12. He was a Spanish poet and religious thinker of the court of Cordova.

13. Author of *Al-Muqaddimah* (An Introduction to History), a socialist, a historian, applied the principles of philosophy to the study of history.

14. A theologians from Damascus, whose life was full of persecution, who was a follower of Ibn Hanbal, and who was credited with the source of Wahhabiyah.

15. An Arab biographer of the Prophet Muhammad (pbuh). His work is considered to be the most important book on the life of the Prophet.

16. Born in Spain, this Arab was celebrated mystic philosopher whose monumental work includes *Al-Futuhat Al-Makkiyah* (The Makkan Revelation).

Exegetes, Exegesis

1. This person is considered to be the first exegete of the Qur'ān.

2. A commentary of the Qur'ān based purely upon personal opinion are generally termed as:

3. This Christian missionary was the first to forge a translation of the Qur'ān in English in his attempt to show that the Qur'ān is 'so manifest a forgery.'

4. One of the earliest and most extensive tafsīr of the Qur'ān. It has 30 volumes and it is the source for all later commentaries.

5. This person is the commentator of one of the well-known tafsīr on the mu'tazila approach, named *Al-Kashshāf*.

6. A tafsīr titled *Tafsīr al-Kabir* is a methodical work of this commentator.

7. A summary of Zamakhsharī's work with additional comments was produced under a title *Anwar Al-Tanzil*. Who was the commentator?

8. Abū 'Ala Maudūdī produced one of the contemporary tafsīr of the Qur'ān. What is the title of his work?

9. The general name of one of the widely read tafsīr. It discusses the chain of narrations and titled *Tafsīr al-Qur'ān al-Azim*.

10. Sayyid Qutb produced one of the contemporary exegeses of the Qur'ān. What is the title of his work?

11. This person wrote the tafsīr titled *Jami al-Bayan fee Tafsīr al-Qur'ān*.

12. *Tafsīr al-Manar* is another excellent commentary of the Qur'ān. Whose work is this?

13. A type of tafsīr generally based on indications but not based on accepted sciences of tafsīr, therefore such tafsīr are not acceptable. What are they called?

14. His work *Itqan fi 'ulum al-Qur'ān* (Mastery in the Sciences of the Qur'ān) is a well-known work on Qur'ānic exegesis. Whose work was it?

15. The term defines a particular approach adopted in the interpretation of the Qur'ān based on reasoning.

16. A Hungarian scholar who traced the development of tafsīr through several stages. Most of the modern academic work on tafsīr is incomplete without referring to works by this person.

44

Answers on page 106

Dynasty

1. Rightly guided Khalifās were followed by this dynasty. What was that dynasty?

2. In Iran Reza Khan was credited to have built this dynasty. What was the name of the dynasty?

3. This political and religious dynasty claimed some connection with the daughter of the Prophet. What was the dynasty?

4. Saladin founded this dynasty in the name of his father. It ruled Egypt and most of 'Irāq, Yemen and Syria in the late 12th and early 13th century.

5. During which dynasty Islam was formally established as a religion in Spain?

6. The Ismaili Shī'ites formed this dynasty in Egypt that established famous Al-Azhar University. What was the dynasty?

7. This tribal group enhanced the downfall of the Abbasid dynasty when they sacked Baghdad.

8. This person is credited to have formed the Spanish Ummayad dynasty in Cordoba.

9. When the Fātimid Dynasty was in power in Egypt, another Shī'ite dynasty controlled Persia and Iraq. What was that dynasty?

10. A dynasty consisting of mostly Turkish nomadic people who moved down from Central Asia.

11. A dynasty that ruled Egypt and Syria, their name derived from Arabic word for "slave" since the slaves gained power and ruled the country.

12. The Shī'ite dominance during the Fātimid and Buyid dynasty was finally driven out of the Syria-Palestine and Arabian Peninsula by this dynasty that was staunch Sunnis.

13. At the time of Ottomans golden age, this dynasty was founded in the beginning of sixteenth century in North India.

14. A sixteenth century dynasty in Persia that established Shī'ite Islam as the state religion.

15. A Turkish dynasty founded by Sabūktagin, a Turkish slave, ruled over Khorasan, Afghanistan and Northern India.

Terminology – I

1. What is the Arabic term for innovation in the name of religion?

2. What is the term used to mean exemption tax paid by the non-Muslims in return for military protection in an Islamic state?

3. What is the term for one of the four legitimate schools of Islamic jurisprudence?

4. What is the term used to mean "consensus" of the Muslim community that gives legitimacy to a legal issue?

5. This word collectively denotes the rule of the four rightly guided Caliphs, who were immediate successor of the Prophet.

6. This term stands for circumambulating the Ka'bah during Hajj.

7. As the name signifies, they were the white garbed followers of 'Isā. What is the term?

8. The word means temptation or trial. The word used to describe civil wars during the Caliphate years and early Umayyad period.

9. What is the term for exercise of independent judgment in Islamic law.

10. What is the term for lesser pilgrimage that can be made at any time?

11. What is the term for optional salāt performed at late night after waking up from sleep?

12. What is the term used to denote oneness of Allāh?

13. What is the term used to describe pre Islamic Age of Ignorance or Age of Darkness?

14. During Hajj, it is customary to pronounce *Labbayek Allāhumma Labbayek* (At your service O Lord, At your service). What is the name or term given to this practice?

15. The term originally meant 'raids' undertaken by Arabs in the pre-Islamic period

16. The term stands for the protected subject in the Islamic empires, who were allowed full religious freedom but were required to recognize Islamic sovereignty.

Terminology – II

1. What is the term for formal legal opinion given by a religious scholar on a matter of Islamic issues?

2. What is the term for remembrance of Allāh especially by means of chanting His name, a way of Sufi devotion?

3. What is the term used to identify the followers of the Companions of the Prophet?

4. The term refers to the rule of correct pronunciation, speed of reading and correct emphasis on the vowels.

5. What is the process of relating the chain of narrators of Hadīth going back to the original narrator?

6. What is the second call for salāt, recited immediately before starting the obligatory salāt?

7. A collection of ancient Jewish writings, consisting of rabbinic ideas, images and lore that became their important secondary religious book.

8. Arabic term used for the biography of the Prophet or his Companions.

9. A sacrifice offered by the parents of a newborn child, particularly to name the child.

10. One-piece head-to-toe veils worn by many Muslim women.

11. What is the term normally used to describe a weak Hadīth?

12. What is the term used to signify inimitability of the Qur'ān?

13. The term stands for uprising of the Palestinian against terrorism and tyranny of the Israeli government.

14. This term defines the main text of the Hadīth.

15. This term defines uncritical and blind imitation of recognized authorities in the area of legal and theological matter.

16. Literally means 'wedding', normally saint's festival held on the anniversary of his death.

17. What is the term for a command which is imperative upon all Muslims but if some people in a group respond to it, the obligation is considered fulfilled.

Terminology – III

1. What is the Persian or Indian term for the Arabic word rasūl or nabi?

2. What is the term for a small book stand, usually used to place the Qur'ān during recitation?

3. What is the Arabic word for a person who knows a lot, a learned or a scholar?

4. What is the Arabic term for a person who is an attorney or an agent?

5. This term signifies wedding feast or breakfast given on the occasion of marriage.

6. This term is used to denote daily lesson or portion of the Qur'ān to be read by a Muslim.

7. This term literally means to cut or divide, but in Islamic terminology it is used to mean animal slaughtered according to the law.

8. According to some report, by the time the Prophet passed away, he left behind 144,000 of Muslims. What is the Arabic term to identify them?

9. This term means 'an atom' or tiny particle. Whoever does an atom's weight of good or bad will see it. What is the term?

10. What is the term for an odd number of prayer, usually added to the salātul 'Ishā.

11. What is the term for a spring to be found in the Paradise. Immortal boys will go round about them.

12. What is the term for formal announcement at which prayer starts?

13. What is the term for Preserved Tablet, a term mentioned only once in the Qur'ān?

14. When a person stands up for salāt, he or she makes a vow or intention. What is it called?

15. What is the term for an estate or property for which zakāt must be paid?

16. What is the term for dissolving a marriage if husband accuses wife of adultery but cannot bring evidence.

17. What is the term for marriage contracted for a limited time, for a certain sum of money, a practice still legal with Shī'ahs?

Answers on page 107

Cities, Countries

1. The general name for the region of western Saudi Arabia, along the Red Sea coast that contains the two holiest cities of Islam.

2. A highland area in the southwestern Saudi Arabia, a Christian deputation from this place came and debated with Muhammad.

3. The expedition of Tabūk was sent to counter a possible attack by this empire.

4. Al-Jazeera, the sensational major news channel is based in this country.

5. Isfahan, Shīrāz, Mashhad and Abādān are cities in this Islamic country.

6. It is traditionally believed that the Great Deluge at the time of Nūh occurred in this country.

7. Although the Salafiyaan movement started in Paris, it proliferated in this Muslim country.

8. It used to be the only Marxist Middle Eastern country. Its capital is Sana.

9. The first Muslim settlement in Indonesia started in the 13th century C.E. on this island.

10. Bander Seri Begawan is the capital of this tiny country that is undergoing increasing Islamization.

11. Baluch, Pathan, Sindhis and Punjabis are the major ethnic groups in this country.

12. A central Asian country, with more than 80% Muslim population, has its capital at Bishkek.

13. This country sandwiched between Libya and Algeria was once the host of PLO during its early years.

14. Khosrow was the king of this country, Salmān belonged to it. What was the country?

15. Bilāl came from this country, and Jaʿfar sought asylum here. What was that country?

16. Muʿawiah moved out of Arabia and established the capital of his caliphate in this city. The city contributed significantly to the Islamic history. Which was the city?

Clue Words - I

(Three or four clue words are given without additional details. Connect the words to the story)

1. Basket, river, sister.

2. Ark, deluge, pair of animals.

3. Well, Egypt, dream.

4. 30 nights plus 10 other, mountain.

5. Hamstrung, brother, sign.

6. Burning brand, mountain.

7. Guests, roasted food, prophecy.

8. Guests, take my daughters.

9. Court, cast, swallow.

10. Nakedness, leaves, clothing.

11. Golden throne, jinn, Yemen.

12. Great monarch, Big wall, Ya'jūj-Ma'jūj.

13. Infant son, water fountain, running around.

14. Cave, Abū Bakr, spider.

15. Negotiation, pilgrimage, 10 year truce.

16. Coats of mail, metal, prophet.

Clue Words - II

(Three or four clue words are given without additional details. Connect the words to the story)

1. Labbayek – aswad – Arafat.

2. Brawl – blow – kill.

3. Thaur – spider – Quba.

4. Mountain– fire – burning brand.

5. Mountain – song – iron.

6. Dream – bread – bird.

7. Disgusted – ship – evil omen.

8. Herd of animals – water – rouges – women.

9. Breakfast – fish – junction of sea.

10. Eastern place– palm tree – ripe dates.

11. Blind – disturbed – turned face.

12. Cup – sack – steal.

13. Elephant – confusion – pelting.

14. Night – thousand months – Angles.

15. Two hands – firewood – twisted rope.

16. Pilgrimage – treaty – clear victory.

Who Said – I

1. I am better than he, You have created me of fire, while You created him of clay.

2. How is it that I do not see Hūd Hūd, or is he among the absentees?

3. O my son! Surely I have seen in the dream that I should sacrifice you, so consider what you see.

4. Wherefrom will there be a son to me, while no man has yet touched me and I have not been unchaste?

5. This is my staff, I lean on it and I beat down leaves with it for my sheep and I have in it other uses.

6. My Rabb! Wherefrom will there be a boy to me, while my wife is barren and I have already grown decrepit from old age?

7. Go with this shirt of mine and shed it before my father's face, he will come to discern. And bring me your family all together.

8. I do not know for you any deity besides myself. Therefore, O Hāmān! Burn a kiln of bricks for me then build for me a tower so that I may rise towards the God.

9. My Rabb! I indeed killed a man of them; therefore I fear they may kill me.

10. O Allāh! Our Rabb! Send down upon us a Table Spread with food from Heaven that it may be to us an Eid for the first of us and for the last of us.

11. O My Father! Why do you worship that which do not hear and do not see, nor can it avail you anything?

12. Oh My dad, surely I have seen eleven stars and the sun and the moon making obeisance for me.

13. You have adjudged me erring. I will certainly lie in ambush for them.

14. Step in to the palace. It is indeed a palace paved smooth with slabs of glass.

15. I shall cut off your hands and your legs on the opposite sides, and I shall crucify you on the trunk of a date tree.

16. If he stole then surely his brother stole before.

Who Said – II

1. These are my guests therefore do not disgrace me.

2. Oh my people! Enter the holy land which Allāh has ordained for you, and do not turn on your backs, for then you will turn back losers.

3. My Rabb! I do hereby dedicate to you what is within my womb, so accept from me, surely You, only You are the all-Hearing, the all-Knowing.

4. Did I not tell you that you would never be able to have patience with me?

5. O son of my mother! Do not seize by my beard or by my head.

6. I believe that there is no deity but He on whom the Children of Israel believe, and I am of the surrenderers.

7. If you laugh at us then surely we will laugh at you just as you are laughing.

8. And do not diminish the measure and the balance, surely I see you well-to-do, and surely I fear for you the chastisement of an all-encompassing day.

9. Make his stay honorable. It may be that he will be of benefit to us, or that we may adopt him as a son.

10. Our Rabb! Surely I have settled some of my offspring in a valley without having agriculture, near your Sacred House.

11. I shall soon take shelter on a mountain; it will protect me from the water.

12. Now send one of you with this silver of yours to the city, then let him find out which is the purest food.

13. Bring me molten copper that I may pour over it.

14. I fled from you when I feared you; now my Rabb has granted me wisdom, and He has made me of the Rasūls.

15. O you Chiefs! An honorable letter has indeed been delivered to me.

16. O my son! Do not associate with Allāh. Surely polytheism is indeed a grievous wrongdoing.

17. My Rabb! Surely my son is from my family and surely your promise is the truth. You are the most Just of the Judges.

 Answers on page 110

Who Said – III

1. I surely I seek refuge from you with the Rahman, if you be reverent.

2. Surely I am a bondsman of Allāh. He has given me the scripture, and He has made me a nabi, And He has made me a blessed one wherever I be, and He has enjoined on me Salat and Zakat so long as I live.

3. My sons! Do not enter by a single gate, but you enter by different gates.

4. I will certainly come upon them from their front and from their back and from their right and from their left.

5. My Rabb! Grant me protection and grant me a kingdom which is not fit for anyone after me.

6. You will certainly never be able to have patience with me.

7. Should you stretch your hand to kill me, I am not going to stretch my hand to kill you. Surely I fear Allāh – the Rabb of the worlds.

8. O You Chiefs! Advise me regarding my affair. I have never decided an affair until you bear witness to me.

9. What has turned them from their Qiblah on which they were?

10. Surely Allāh is going to test you by a river, so whoever drinks from it, he is not of my followers, but whoever does not taste he is then my follower.

11. My Rabb! I have surely done wrong to myself and I submit with Sulaimān to Allāh, the Rabb of all worlds.

12. Glory be to you! We have no knowledge except what you have taught us.

13. But Allāh brings out the sun from the East, so you bring it from the West.

14. Oh good gracious! Here is a boy!

15. Indeed I saw I carry on my head a loaf, birds were eating from it.

16. The bones in me are weakened and the head flares with hoariness, and my Rabb! Never have I been unsuccessful in my prayer to you.

17. If his shirt is torn at the back, then she has told lies and he is of the truthful.

Places in the Qur'ān

(note: these places may not have been mentioned by name in the Qur'ān)

1. Ancient name of Madīnah, people from which came to invite Muhammad (pbuh).

2. Before the Qiblah was set to Makkah, this was the Qiblah for Muslims.

3. During the early years of Islam, some followers migrated to this Christian country.

4. People from this city pelted stones and ridiculed Muhammad (pbuh) when he went there to preach Islam.

5. Mūsā lived in this deserted wilderness for 8 to 10 long years and got married.

6. Prophet Yūsuf lived in this country where he was granted a senior position in the kingdom.

7. Masjid An-Nabawi or the Prophet's mosque is located in this city.

8. Only 313 companions of Muhammad (pbuh) engaged in a battle in this place.

9. A famous battle was fought at this place, where Muslims suffered a lot due to archers negligence and the Prophet nearly died.

10. First oath of allegiance was taken by 12 men from Yathrib at this place.

11. The Ark of Nūh landed in this place.

12. The longest expedition mentioned in sūrah Taubah (aka Bārat).

13. A Christian deputation that came from this place was challenged by the Prophet to pray for death in order to ascertain truth.

14. Dhu al-Qurnain reached this place where the sun was setting in this place. What was the place?

15. A biblical town by the seashore that violated the Sabbath when they went to catch fish.

16. In the land of Palestine this city was destroyed twice due to mischief of the Israelites.

17. Badr is located slightly outskirts of Madīnah. Using mileage scale, how far is Badr from Madīnah?

Islamic History – I

1. How many years after the Hijrah did the conquest of Makkah occur?

2. Who was the Indian poet and philosopher who emphasized rationality in Islam and tried to prove it was quite compatible with Western modernity.

3. He was a Pakistani religious ideologue, commentator of the Qur'ān, founder of a political party. Who was he?

4. The most magnificent Abbasid Caliph, whose reign coincided with the zenith of caliphal absolute power.

5. Who was the last of the prominent Mughal emperor, a devout Muslim, who ruled for about 50 years and ruled almost entire India, unprecedented by any former Mughal emperors?

6. Which prophet was the immediate forerunner of 'Isa?

7. This journalist who founded the Salafiyyah movement in Cairo and was the first to advocate fully modernized Islamic state.

8. He was a theologian from Baghdad, he gave a definitive expression to Sunni Islam, and brought Sufism into the mainstream of piety.

9. Egyptian scholar and commentator of the Qur'ān, ordered to be executed by Al-Nasser's regime for his ideology.

10. A prominent Umayyad family member, who bitterly opposed the Prophet but later accepted Islam when Makkah fell.

11. A great Muslim mathematician and astronomer, who invented logarithms and wrote a book, from which modern Algebra is derived.

12. What two events marked the "Year of Sadness"?

13. In which Islamic year the direction of the Qiblah was changed from Masjid Al-Aqsa to Masjid al-Haram?

14. In this year the Caliphate was finally abolished.

15. The Muslim conquest of Spain was lead by this person in the year 711 C.E.

16. The Golden Age of medieval Iraq was culminated with this Caliphate.

Answers on page 111

Islamic History – II

1. The most romanticized tales of The Thousand and One Night is associated with this Caliph.

2. This Muslim person was the scribe in the Treaty of Hūdaibiyah.

3. The Hijri calendar starts from the year the Prophet migrated from Makkah to Madīnah. Who established the Hijri calendar?

4. Ja'far recited the beginning of this sūrah to the king of Abyssinia to convince him to let the Muslims stay in his country.

5. Which Abbasid Caliph strictly imposed Mu'tazili doctrine advocating free will and full human responsibility

6. Harun al-Rashid was a Caliph of the Abbasid Empire, to which empire did Ma'mun al-Rashid belong?

7. Abū Lahab succumbed to his head injury when this woman cracked a wooden post on his head as a protest against beating a new Muslim in her own house.

8. How many years of peace were agreed upon by the Treaty of Hūdaibiyah?

9. Who did the Quraish sent to conduct and sign the Treaty of Hūdaibiyah?

10. Babur was the first Muslim king of an Islamic empire that ruled for nearly 300 years? What was the empire?

11. About five hundred years before Mughal Empire was established in India, this Muslim first invaded India. Who was he?

12. This legendary Muslim king in India first established postal system and built a major highway covering east and west of India,which is still being used. Who was the king?

13. Battle of Camel was fought between 'Ali and this person. Who was the person?

14. Ancient city of Ghazni was famous during medieval period. In which country Ghazni is located?

15. Taj Mahal is a mausoleum built by a Mughal emperor in memory of his wife. Who was the emperor?

16. Which country did the Tughlaq, Lodhi and Khilji rulers rule in the medieval period?

Communities, Nations, Tribes, Emperors

1. This clan by the name of "Banu - " showed tremendous revulsion towards Muhammad (pbuh) and the new Muslims during the early years of Islam.

2. The Israelites are mostly addressed as Banu Israel in the Qur'ān. What term is used to describe the Christians?

3. Three Jewish tribes were determined to destroy the Prophet by doing various conspiracies against him. Two were Banu Qurayzah and Banu Nadīr. Which was the third tribe?

4. The people of these two tribes in Madīna converted to Islam and became known as 'ansars.'

5. This tribe lived inside the territory of Madīnah. They were expelled in 2 A.H. for their opposition of Islam.

6. Mūsā was instructed to find streams for his tribes by striking rocks. How many tribes were with him for whom he found streams?

7. In sūrah # 106, this tribe is said to have worshipped the Lord of the House for blessing them in many ways.

8. This ancient Arabian tribe lived south of Arabia, in the Hadramauth region. The lost city of Iram was built by them. Who were they?

9. The Prophet led 25 days blockade against this Jewish tribe in Madinah for their braking treaty of neutrality with the Muslims in the battle of Uhud.

10. Which nation held the Children of Israel in bondage for about 400 years?

11. A great nation of the past that worshipped sun, and its ruler was a woman, mentioned in in the Qur'ān.

12. Which country was ruled by a king who dreamt about seven cows?

13. Who was the Roman emperor against whom the Prophet undertook the Expedition of Tabuk?

14. Who was the emperor mentioned in the Qur'ān that traveled to the land where sun sets in black sea?

15. Which Persian king was defeated by the Romans in the year 628 C.E., a prophecy of which was indicated in sūrah Ar-Rum?

16. A prophet asked this emperor to bring the sun from the west. Who was that emperor?

Answers on page 111

Wives of the Prophet

1. The first convert to Islam was one of the Prophet's wives. Who was she?

2. Miscreants spread a slander against this wife of Muhammad (pbuh).

3. Rich merchant lady, of the clan of Asad, was one of the wives of the Prophet Muhammad (pbuh).

4. She was 'Umar's daughter, a dignified wife of the Prophet Muhammad (pbuh).

5. After adopted son Zaid divorced this woman, the Prophet married her. Who was she?

6. She was wife of Al-'Abbās, also a cousin of the Prophet. When she became widow, the Prophet married her. Who was she?

7. She was daughter of Zamah, also sister of Suhail. After Khadījah died, she was the first woman married by the Prophet.

8. This lady is known by her son's name. When her husband died from the injuries received during the battle of Uhud, both Abū Bakr and 'Umar proposed to marry her, but later the Prophet married her.

9. How long was the Prophet married to his first wife Khadījah?

10. How old was the Prophet when he took multiple numbers of women as his wives?

11. Two wives of the Prophet had the same first name. Who were they?

12. She was the daughter of Al-Hārith. After she was taken as captive during the campaign against the Banu Must'aliq, the Prophet married her.

13. Long before Abū Sufyān converted to Islam, the Prophet married one of his daughters when she divorced her husband who had accepted Christianity.

14. After the battle of Khaybar, the Prophet married one of the Jewish captive women, who happened to be the daughter of the chief of the Banu Nadīr.

15. Her half sister, Zaynab bint Khuzayma, was a wife of the Prophet. Later she herself was married to the Prophet Who was she?

16. This wife of the Prophet saved a copy of the Qur'ān recorded by Zayd ibn Thābit. It eventually became the source of further copies during the time of 'Uthmān.

Hajj

1. How many times a pilgrim must go round Ka'bah During the Hajj, in order to complete Tawāf?

2. As one of the last rites during the Hajj, pilgrims are required to spend one night in this place.

3. Pilgrims wear two seamless clothes are worn during Hajj. When they wear it, they are said to be in the sate of _____. What is that state?

4. If a person were performing Hajj, he would be in this valley on the day of Hajj.

5. Who lead the Hajj on the 9th A.H., one year before the famous Hajj?

6. What are the names of the three pillars in Minā where the pilgrims throw pebbles after returning from Arafāt?

7. The places from which the pilgrims to Makkah assume the state of Ihrām.

8. The term indicates walking seven times between the hills of Safā and Marwah.

9. Which Eid is celebrated at the time of performing the Hajj?

10. During Hajj, a person leaves Arafāt at sunset to reach this place.

11. What rite is done at Jamaraat al-Aqubah?

12. The term defines the rites of being present in the plains of Arafāt.

13. What is the name of the black brocade drape that covers the Ka'bah?

14. What is the name of the famous stone on the east corner of the Ka'bah.

15. The term used to denote chanting during Hajj: *Labbayk Allāhumma labbayk.*

16. Where would one see thousands of pitched white tents during the Hajj?

17. During the Hajj, when do the pilgrims move in counter clockwise direction?

18. During the Hajj what would a pilgrim do with jamrah as-sughra, jamrah al-wusta and jamrat al-`Aqabah?

Answers on page 112

Number

1. According to the Qur'ān how many clear signs were shown by Mūsā?

2. How many verses does the oft-repeated sūrah in the Qur'ān contain?

3. In English calendar we have 12 months. How many months did Allāh prescribe for the Muslims?

4. How many Muslims fought in the Battle of Badr?

5. Approximately how many Muslims accompanied the Prophet when Makkah surrendered?

6. How many sūrahs are said to be revealed in Makkah?

7. How many sūarh starts with abbreviated letters called Muqatta'āt?

8. Between Abū Bakr and 'Ali total of how many years did the Rightly Guided Khalīfahs rule?

9. Total verses in the second largest sūrah in the Qur'ān (clue: As-Shu'arā)

10. How many Muslims accompanied the Prophet for the pilgrimage that ended in signing the Treaty of Hūdaibiyah?

11. How many of the Prophet's children were living at the time when Prophet passed away?

12. Out of twenty-seven books in New Testament, how many are Gospel?

13. As mentioned in the Qur'ān, how many sons did prophet Ya'qūb have?

14. In the same year of Battle of Uhud, a tribe invited Muslims to teach them Islam, but treacherously killed them at Bir Mauna. How many Muslims were killed in the event?

15. What was the age of Fātimah when she died?

16. How many years did the Prophet practice Islam secretly and privately along with his new converts before making it public?

17. How many times the abbreviation Alif Lām Mīm occur as three letter combination in a sūrah?

18. Out of 29 letters in Arabic alphabet, how many letters occur in various combinaitons, called Muqatta'āt in the beginning of some sūrahs?

Year

1. When did the USA declare its independence using the fundamental Islamic principle that all men are created equal?

2. Hijrah marks the beginning of Muslim Calendar, to which C.E. does it correspond to?

3. In the Battle of Badr, fought in this C.E. year, Muslims inflicted dramatic defeat upon the Quraish.

4. What was the year in which Abrahah invaded Makkah with his army of elephants?

5. The Treaty of Hūdaibiyya was signed in this C.E. year.

6. In sūrah al-Ma'ārij Allāh says a day is equivalent to how many years?

7. The six-days war between Israel and its Arab neighbors fought in this year resulted in occupation of the West Bank.

8. Jewish state of Israel was created in this year, forcing 750,000 Palestinians to leave their home land and asking them never to return.

9. In which year Israel and the Palestinians signed the famous Oslo Accord?

10. Holy Prophet was born in the year 570 C.E., in which year was his father born?

11. Until his death in this year, grandfather 'Abdul Muttalib took care of child Muhammad (pbuh).

12. Although the Islamic calendar was started with the Hijrat of the Prophet from Makkah to Madīnah, in which year did the early Muslims undertook the first Hijrat to Abyssinia?

13. The first pledge of Aqaba paved the path of great migration of the Prophet. In which year the pledge took place?

14. After the battle of Uhud, the expedition known as Badr al-Sughra or Minor Badr was undertaken in this year. What was the year in C.E.?

15. The most famous pilgrimage, known as Farewell Pilgrimage was undertaken in this important year. What was the answer in C.E.?

16. In which year the Temple of Jerusalem was destroyed for the 2nd time?

Author

1. The author of "The Message of the Qur'ān."

2. The author of "Even Angels Ask."

3. The author of "Bible, the Qur'ān and Science."

4. The author of "Fi Zilalil Qur'ān."

5. The author of "The Road to Mecca."

6. The author of "Rubayyat."

7. The wrote "Islam and Revolution."

8. The author of "The History of God – 4000 year quest of Judaism, Christianity and Islam."

9. The author of "Muhammad – His life based on the earliest sources."

10. Who wrote "The 100 – A Ranking of The Most Influential Person in History."

11. This congress man from Illinois wrote a sensational book titled "Silent No More."

12. The author of "Itqan fi 'ulum al-Qur'ān."

13. The author of "Muqaddimah," (An Introduction to History).

14. The author of "Tafsīr al-Manar," a famous exegesis of the Qur'ān from Egypt.

15. The editor of "Al-Jami Al-Musnad al-Sahih."

16. The author of The Canon of Medicine (*al-Qanun fi at-tibb*), which is by all means, the most famous single book in the history of medicine in both East and West.

17. He composed *Shāhnāma*, a collection of poems that are widely read today and translated in many languages?

Names of Allāh

1. By general understanding, how many *asma al-husna* does Allāh (swt) have?

2. One of the names of Allāh (swt) means "the Mysterious" or "the Subtle one." What is the name?

3. One of the names of Allāh (swt) meaning "the Mightly" or "the Guardian." What is that name?

4. A qualifying name of Allāh meaning 'the 'Alive.' What is the name?

5. A qualifying name of Allāh meaning 'the governor.' What is the name?

6. A qualifying name of Allāh meaning 'the Guide.' What is the name?

7. A qualifying name of Allāh meaning 'the Reckoner.' What is the name?

8. A qualifying name of Allāh meaning 'the Witness.' What is the name?

9. The meaning of Allāh's qualifying name Al-Wadūd.

10. The meaning of Allāh's qualifying name Al-Kabīr.

11. The meaning of Allāh's qualifying name Al-Khabīr.

12. The meaning of Allāh's qualifying name Ar-Razzāq

13. The meaning of Allāh's qualifying name Al-Quddūs.

14. The meaning of Allāh's qualifying name Al-Fattāh.

15. The meaning of Allāh's qualifying name Al-Azīm.

16. The meaning of Allāh's qualifying name Al-Awwal.

Answers on page 113

Personality

1. In the year 1940 this leader of Muslim League demanded a separate Muslim country be formed for the Muslim population after the British rule ends.

2. This eighteenth century Shah from India is credited with his attempt to reassess Islamic theology in the light of modernity.

3. This poet, philosopher from British India envisioned formation of Pakistan as separate Muslim country.

4. This leader of Nations of Islam, known for civil rights movement. In 1963 he took his followers to mainstream Islam. Who was he?

5. The highest point in the Abbasid Caliphate was reached during the time of this person.

6. To which country the founder of Muslim Brotherhood Hasan al-Banna belong?

7. This British military strategist, in whose name a movie was made, led the Arab attack to destroy the railway track near Hijāz.

8. The greatest medieval Sufi mystic and Persian poet whose followers are called the Whirling Darvishes.

9. This Ummayad Caliph is remembered for his murder near Karbala.

10. About this distinguished historian of all time, Arnold Toynbee said "... undoubtedly the greatest work of its kind that has ever yet been created by any mind in any time or place." Who was he?

11. This scholar from Baghdad is credited for bringing Sufism into mainstream of piety.

12. A Sunni reformer achieved much success when his movement named after him was largely supported by Ibn Saud.

13. This woman was one of the key people during the First Fitnah.

14. Famous medieval Mongol warrior unified Mongol into a formidable nation. Who was he?

15. Egyptian reformer, founder of the Society of Muslim Brothers, assassinated in 1949.

16. In the world of Muslim literary achievement, this person deserves mention for his famous work Muqaddimah.

Contemporary Muslim Personalities
(Period: 1990 -2006)

1. He is a professor of mathematics, a convert into Islam, known for several books on Islam.

2. An Islamic scholar born in Egypt, lived in Qatar. He is kown for his book The Lawful and Prohibited in Islam

3. He was prime minister of Malaysia between 1981 and 2003. He was the architect of modernizing Malaysia yet preserving Islamic values.

4. He was both IBF and WBC World heavyweight boxing champion for seven months after he defeated Lennox Lewis.

5. This NFL football player, with his name very similar to another NBA player, played for Miami Dolphin, Cleveland Browns and Indianapolis Colt.

6. He is NBA Hall of Fame player played for LA Lakers during 1975-1989. He was inducted in the Hall of Fame in 1995. Who is he?

7. He was a famous NBA player, played with Houston Rockets.

8. What was the English name of pop singer who is now known as Yusuf Islam?

9. A German diplomat and director of NATO. When he accepted Islam it created huge uproar in Germany. Who is he?

10. This female associate professor of Islamic studies came into limelight when she led a Friday prayer in 2005. Who was she?

11. He led the Hamas win a landslide election in the year 2006 and sworn in as Prime Minister. Who is he?

12. A leading politician of the Fatah, he was the first Prime Minister of the Palestinian Authority and elected President of PNA in 2005. Who is he?

13. She is the only Muslim woman to win a Nobel prize. She was awarded Peace prize in 2003. Who is she?

14. He won Nobel Prize for literature in 1988. He is known for this famous book Children of Gebelawi.

15. He was England Cricket player and captain of the England team. He represented England team in 2003 Cricket World Cup.

16. This person and his organization won the Nobel Peace Prize in 2006. Name them.

Answers on page 114

Khalīfa, Caliphate

1. This Khalīfa was also the first youngest person to accept Islam.

2. The Caliphate of Harun Al-Rashid is popularly associated with this romanticized tales.

3. In this country the Abbasid Caliphate was largely concentrated.

4. This city was the capital of Eastern Umayyad Dynasty.

5. This city was the capital of Islamic government during the Abbasid Caliphate.

6. Upon assassination of 'Ali, this person became the Khalīfa and founded the Caliphate known as Umayyad Caliphate.

7. The battle of Karbala was staged by this Umayyad Khalīfa.

8. The Second Fitnah in the history of Islamic civilization occurred during this person's Caliphate.

9. Total of how many years did the rule of the Rashidun last?

10. After the death of 'Ali, since no successor was chosen, this person became the Khalīfa for six months then stepped down from the Caliphate.

11. What Baghdad was to the Abbasids, this city was to the Umayyad.

12. This Khalīfa formally established Baghdad as the new capital of the Abbasid Caliphate.

13. The dynastic struggle brought about the end of Caliphate decline. This decline was more enhanced when this tribe destroyed Baghdad.

14. This new Caliphate, known as the Caliphate of Qurtubah, or Caliphate of Cordova was an offshoot of the Abbasid dynasty. Who formed the Caliphate of Cordova?

15. Halaku Khan, grandson of Chengiz Khan overthrew this Caliphate.

16. The Shī'ite Muslims do not prefer to use the title Khalīfas, rather they use this title. What is that?

17. The Abbasid Caliphate used Turkish Muslim slaves as their soldiers. What is the general term used to denote these slave soldiers?

The Only

1. He was the only rightly guided Khalīfa who was not assassinated.

2. The only wife of the Prophet other than Khadījah to bear a child for the Prophet.

3. The only prophet symbolically addressed as friend of Allāh.

4. Technically the only place where a Muslim may pray in any direction yet it would be acceptable.

5. She is the only woman named by her actual name in the Qur'ān.

6. The only prophet adopted in infancy by someone while his mother was still alive.

7. Only one sūrah starts with two sets of abbreviated letters in its first two verses. What is the name of the sūrah?

8. Only two Muslims were featured in the book "The 100 – A Ranking of the Most Influential Person in History". One was our Prophet, ranked # 1; who was the other?

9. What is the only sūrah to bear the name of a community outside of Arabian Peninsula?

10. The only sūrah where the Allāh disapproved the Prophet when his dealing appeared unacceptable.

11. He is the only Companion of the Prophet mentioned by name in the Qur'ān?

12. The only sūrah where the phrase 'bismillāh ar- rahmān ar-rahīm' appear twice.

13. The only sūrah named after a top member of the Prophet's greater family.

14. When was the only time the Prophet traveled to Jerusalem?

15. Other than Sulaimān, he was the only other prophet to make use of birds in his army.

16. Only two sūrahs in the Qur'ān bear single letter title, one is *Qaf* (#50), what is the other.

17. Who is the only grandson of 'Abd Al-Muttalib to become one of the Khalīfas?

Shī'ite Islam

1. This person was briefly served as the fifth Khalīfa as well as the second Imam.

2. This person, a close companion of the Prophet, was considered to be the first Imam in Shī'ite Islam.

3. This person, governor of Syrian province, contested the appointment of the fifth Khalīfa.

4. A decisive rupture between the Sunnis and the Shī'ites originated from this incident.

5. The martyrdom of Hussain, the grand son of the Prophet, occurred in this place that became one of the holiest shrines of the Shī'ite Islam.

6. This sect is the largest and the most recognized sect of the Shī'ite Islam.

7. He was the very controversial figure, a young son, recognized as the twelfth Imam in Shī'ite Islam.

8. One of the Shī'ite Imams went into seclusion and never appeared in public; thus, this term symbolically identifies him.

9. The Shī'ite Islam predicts that one of their Imams would reappear in the later time as "Mahdi". Who is that Imam?

10. Some of the members of the Shī'ite Islam are not the 'Twelvers' they are the 'Seveners'. What is their other name?

11. The Ismā'īli Shī'ite Islam considers that they had only seven Imams, as 'Ali's line ended with this person.

12. According to Shī'ite Islam, the hidden and true meaning of the Qur'ānic revelation can be known through this designated person. What is the designation?

13. In which month the Shī'ite Islam observe the passion play or Ta'zīyah where self-flagellation and breast-beating takes place to commemorate the sacrifice in Karbala?

14. An important branch of the Ismā'īli Shī'ites settled in Cairo in 909 C.E. and formed a dynasty named after a member of the Prophet. What is that dynasty?

15. The Fātimid Ismā'īli Shī'ites produced this small group, currently located in Syria and Lebanon.

Denominations & Sects

1. A crisis relating to this issue brought about the formation of the Sunnis and Shī'ites—the two major sects in Islam.

2. Although the Sunnis constitute the four fifth of the Muslim population, during one dynasty most of the world Muslims were Shī'ites. Which was the dynasty?

3. Zayd, the son of the fourth Twelver Imam, formed this denomination of the Shī'ite Islam, currently concentrated in Yemen.

4. This denomination first emerged after the battle of Siffin when they objected to 'Ali's seeking arbitration.

5. A sect originated from the Twelver Shī'ites in the tenth century Baghdad, dominant in Syria, they deify 'Ali and believe in transmigration of souls.

6. An offshoot of Ismā'īlism, considered fully independent of mainstream Islam. They consider Fātimid Khalīfa al-Hakim was divine. The faith is mostly kept under secrecy from outer world.

7. The leader of this denomination takes the title Bahaullah or Glory of Allāh.

8. What is the religious movement originated in nineteenth century India in the name of Mirza Ghulam Ahmad, with followers all over the world?

9. Wallace Fard founded this denomination in 1930 in Detroit. They considered Fard as God and his successors also as prophets.

10. This denomination living mostly in Lebanon, Israel and Syria are numbered more than 250,000. This is astonishing since they permit no conversion either away from or to their religion, and no intermarriage.

11. What Elijah Muhammad was to the Nations of Islam, this person was to the Qadianis.

12. The Twelver Shī'ites gave rise to this sect in the nineteenth century Iran. They are considered outside the pale of Islam but spread in India, Europe and USA.

13. This person brought followers of the Nations of Islam into a new group and brought them closer to true Islam.

14. A prominent African American Muslim, who was a follower of Nations of Islam philosophy, but later turned into an orthodox Muslim.

Crime and Punishment

1. What punishment did Abū Jahl receive at the battle of Badr for opposing the Muslims?

2. What punishment did Banu Quraizah receive for betraying the Prophet?

3. After Mūsā accidentally killed an Egyptian, what punishment was he afraid of?

4. What punishment did youngest brother of Yūsuf receive for alleged crime of stealing king's cup?

5. How many years did Yūsuf languish in the prison for the false crime of seducing a women?

6. What punishment did the Prophet give to those Muslims who refused to go to the Expedition of Tabūk?

7. What specific punishment inflicted the community of prophet Lūt for defying the divine teachings?

8. What punishment did people impose upon Ibrāhīm for his preaching monotheism?

9. When some of the magicians accepted Islam, what punishment did Fir'awn threaten them with?

10. What punishment is prescribed in the Qur'ān for the crime of adultery?

11. In order to establish the crime of adultery, how many witnesses are required?

12. When the Christian deputation from Najrān refused to acknowledge truth in Islam, what punishment did the Prophet asked them to seek?

13. When Banu Nadīr broke the treaty of neutrality, what punishment was imposed upon them according to the teachings of Tawrat?

14. In order to atone for accidental killing of a person, the killer is required to compensate the deceased person's family with something. What is this procedure called?

15. When a Muslim abandons his religion and accepts other religion, what punishment can Muslims impose upon the person?

16. What punishment does the Qur'ān prescribe for a habitual thief?

Title

1. The Qur'ān refers to him as *Rūhu'l-Amīn*. Who is he?

2. The Prophet gave Abū Bakr a special title. What is that title?

3. What title is given to the sūrah Fātihah? The title is also used for the Qur'ān.

4. This place is referred to as *Ummu'l Qura*. What is that place?

5. In the Qur'ān in 4:125 *Khalīlu'llāh* is a title given to a person. Who is the person?

6. In battle of Uhud he was an enemy, but later he was given the title 'The Sword of Allāh'. Who was he?

7. *Ummul Mu'minīn* is an title given to these people.

8. The title 'Cat Father' or 'The Kitten Man' was used to identify this man.

9. Which animal is often referred to in the Qur'ān as a Symbol of Allāh?

10. This item placed on the sacrificial camels is called Symbol of Allāh.

11. The Qur'ān and the Torah, both are referred to by this symbolic title.

12. Due to his reddish complexion he was called Abū Lahab. What was his proper name?

13. According to a Hadīth *Kalīmu'llāh* title applies to a prophet. Who is he?

14. Due to his extreme arrogance and ignorance, this person was called Abū Jahl or Father of Ignorance.

15. Dhu an-Nūn is a title given to a prophet. Who is the prophet?

16. According to a Hadīth, this person is *Ruhu'llāh*.

17. When Abbasid Caliphate came in power, they created a bureaucratic position and delegated administrative power to them. What was the title given to the position?

Parables

1. In a parable, the Qur'ān says this creature builds the flimsiest of the house.

2. Allāh is not ashamed to strike a parable of something as small as this.

3. In the parable of those who spend in charity, how many ears does a grain grow into?

4. In the parable of those who spend in charity, how many grains grow in each ear?

5. In a parable of believer who spends in the path of Allāh is like a garden upon which heavy rain falls, but if there is no rain, what is said to be sufficient?

6. In a parable of disbeliever, they are compared to this thing that does not have soil, so heavy rain makes it barren.

7. Those who disbelieve, their parable are like this thing in a desert.

8. The parable of the deeds of disbeliever is like this item upon which wind blows on a stormy day—thus the deed gets lost.

9. The parable of the Rabbis who carry the Tawrat but do to adhere to its teachings is likened with this. What is it?

10. The parable of one that rejects the truth is like this animal that lolls out his tongue if you chase him out or leave him alone.

11. In sūrah An-Nūr, what item is used to illustrate the parable of light?

12. Mountain would crumble due to fear of Allāh if this were sent to it. What is that thing?

13. In the parable of evil world it is compared to an evil tree. What happens to it?

14. In the parable of a rich man in sūrah Al-Kahf, he was given two gardens enclosed by date palms. What type of garden was that?

15. In a parable in sūrah At-Taubah, where does a disbeliever build the foundation of his house?

16. In a parable what does this woman breaks after spinning it strong.

Brothers, Sisters

1. This brother was dragged by his beard for allegedly misleading the Israelites.

2. This person is guilty of killing his brother and hiding the body until a crow reveled the crime.

3. The elders fondly referred to her as Sister of Hārūn. Who was she?

4. Asma's younger sister became one of the *ummul mu'minīn*. Who was she?

5. This brother was held prisoner in Egypt for an alleged crime of stealing.

6. How many brothers conspired to kill Yūsuf or abandon in a well?

7. This youngest brother of Abū Lahab was the grandfather of Fātimah.

8. This red complexioned brother of Abū Tālib was one of the fiercest opponents of the Prophet.

9. They were the elder sisters of Fātimah, the wives of 'Uthmān Ibn Affan.

10. He is the elder brother of prophet Ya'qūb's father. Who was he?

11. They were the mankind's two earliest brothers. Who were they?

12. He was a martyr in Uhud. He was the brother of the Prophet's father. Who was he?

13. Ja'far had a brother who later became a Khalifa. Who was that brother?

14. 'Abdullāh ibn Jahsh wanted their sister to marry the Prophet. But the Prophet did not marry her until she was married to someone and divorced by the man. Who was the sister?

15. Maimūnah was one of the wives of the Prophet. One of her cousin sister was also the Prophet's wife. Who was she?

16. Āminah and 'Abdullah were the Prophet's parents. Who was 'Abdullah sister?

Answers on page 117

Father and Forefather

1. The Qur'ān speaks about father of Ibrāhīm. What was his name?

2. The Prophet's grandfather was a leader of the Quraish. Who was he?

3. Like the son, his father also knew a lot about birds. Who was the father?

4. This father worshipped for three days and three nights as sign sent by Allāh. Who was he?

5. Who was Ya'qūb's father?

6. He was father of Hamza, Abū Lahab and Abū Tālib. Who was he?

7. Who was the great grand father of Yūsuf?

8. Ths son of Abū Tālib was known as "father of the Poor". He was myrtyred at the battle of Mu'tah.

9. Al-'Abbās had a son who was a great commentator of the Qur'ān. Who was he?

10. Who was the maternal great grandfather of Hasan and Husayn?

11. Who sent a shirt to his father as a token of his remembrance?

12. In the Qur'ān a father advised all his sons not to die unless they are Muslims. Who was that father?

13. The adopted son divorced his wife, but his foster father married the divorced woman. This account is mentioned in sūrah Ahzāb. Who was the foster father?

14. This adopted son divorced his wife, but his foster father married the divorced woman. This account is mentioned in sūrah Ahzāb. Who was the adopted son?

15. This son told his father to do what he had been commanded, for he was ready.

16. Umm Habiba was a wife of the Prophet, but father did not believe in Islam for a long time, rather he was a vicious enemy of the Prophet. Who was that father?

17. Who told his father he did not care, he could climb upon a mountain and save himself?

Common

(not the most obvious answer – but the most distinguishing characteristics)

1. What is common with Karen Armstrong, Martin Ling and Ibn Ishaq?

2. When it comes to books, what is common with Rodwell, George Sale, A. J. Arberry?

3. What is common with Nasā'ī, Ibn Mājah and Abū Dāwūd?

4. What is common with Lāt, Manāt and 'Uzza?

5. What is common with Mālik, Hārūt, Nakīr, Munkar?

6. What is common with Hamza, Abū Tālib and Abū Lahab?

7. What is common between Khadījah and Maria, other than them being wives of the Prophet?

8. What is common with Yazīd I, Abdul Mālik, 'Umar II and Yazīd II?

9. What is common with An-Nūr, Al-Karīm, Al Hudā, Al-Kalām?

10. What is common with 'Uthman, 'Umar and 'Ali, but not with Abū Bakr?

11. With regards to the Prophet, what is common with 'Ali and 'Uthman, but cannot be said if Abū Bakr and 'Umar are included?

12. With regards to the Prophet, what is common with Abū Bakr and 'Umar, but cannot be said if 'Ali and 'Uthman are included?

13. What is common with Jahīm, Hutamah, Laza, Hāwiyah?

14. What is common with Al-Burhān, Al-Furqān, Ash-Shifā' Al-Hikmah?

15. What is common with Zayd Ibn Thābit, Abdullah Ibn Al-Zubair, Said Ibn Al-'Ās and Abdul-Rahman Ibn Al-Hārith Ibn Hishām.

16. What is common with locust, plague, draught, frog, lice, blood?

17. Shī'ah Muslims belonging to different denominations believe in different number of Imams. How many Imams are common among all denominations?

 Answers on page 117

The Qur'ān and the Bible

1. The Qur'ān does not support this theory but according to the Bible, this prophet built lots of idols and sculptures and reverted to idol worshipping in his later age.

2. The Qur'ān is silent about it, but the Bible indicates this prophet was beheaded at the order of king Herod to appease a courtesan.

3. The Qur'ān clearly rejects this claim made in the Bible that this father admonished his son for a dream.

4. The Bible blames this woman for misleading her husband, the Qur'ān does not.

5. The Bible says you shall not worship no other god for the Lord is a J* god. What is word for J*?

6. The Bible says this woman looked back and was turned into a pillar of salt, the Qur'ān says she stayed back.

7. The Bible does not like this prophet due to allegation that his birth was from an unwedded mother; however, the Qur'ān highly regards him.

8. The Bible says this prophet was dumbstruck for three days, the Qur'ān simply says he maintained silence for three days and three nights.

9. According to the Bible, this prophet abandoned his wife in a desert, but Qur'ān does not say he abandoned them. Who was the prophet?

10. About the Angels, the Bible says they are ____, the Qur'ān strictly rejects this notion.

11. The Qur'ān has 114 chapters, how many 'books' does the Bible have?

12. The Qur'ān says Zabūr was sent to Dāwūd. In which chapter in the Bible Zabūr is compiled?

13. King James Authorized Version of the Bible is considered to be the accurate Bible. In which century this Authorized Version was produced?

14. In which chapter in the Bible the dietary laws to the Jews were prescribed?

15. Jesus never taught Christianity, it was another person who made up the religion in the name of Christ. Who was he?

16. The first chapter in the Bible is Genesis, which is the second chapter?

Ladies in the Qur'ān

(Note: The Qur'ān may not have mentioned the ladies by their name).

1. She was the legendary lady ruler at Yemen, eventually surrendered to a king and became a Muslim. Who was she?

2. Mother of a prophet to whom angels brought the message of birth of a child.

3. Mother of Ishāq, an old woman, who smiled when prophecy of birth of a child was made to her.

4. This mother was scared for the life of her son, yet she cast her son in the river. Who was she?

5. Wife of a notorious Egyptian ruler was a righteous woman. What was her name?

6. When Zaid divorced this woman, the Prophet married her. Who was she?

7. Zakariyyāh took care of this woman during her childhood. Who was she?

8. This woman was identified as the daughter of Imrān and also as Sister of Hārūn.

9. Wives of two different prophets were unbelievers and not saved, one was Nūh's wife, and the other was this wife. Who was she?

10. After a tricky situation with this lady of the house, a prophet languished several years in jail. Who was she?

11. The unbelievers spread scandal against this lady during her return from an expedition against Banu Mustaliq. Who was she?

12. About whom was said: 'these are my daughters, they are purer for you.'

13. This lady was in grief, she smote her face and expressed that she was an old barren woman.

14. This woman adopted one of the prophets, but the prophet was not Yūsuf.

15. This lady invited several other elite ladies of the city for a feast in her house.

16. About whom it was told that they could opt for the life of this world and its adornments and consequently part a noble parting.

17. Who entered a palace by slightly lifting her skirt so that the skirt may no get wet from the water?

Answers on page 118

The Difference

1. Of all the sūrahs in the Qur'ān, sūrah Taubah is different in one way. What is the difference?

2. How is masjid-ul Qiblatain different from other mosques?

3. Of all the mosques in Arabia, the mosque in Quba is different in one way. What is the main difference?

4. The Adhān for fajr prayer is different from the Adhān for other prayers. What is the specific difference?

5. Salātul Janazah is different from other regular salāt. There are several differences. What is the main difference?

6. When it comes to interacting with non-believers, Muharram, Rajab, Dhul Qa'dah and Dhul Hajjah are different from other months in Islamic calendar. What is the difference?

7. Of all the wives of the Prophet, 'Ā'ishah is different in one way. The answer is not she was a child. What is the answer?

8. When it comes to marriage relationship, 'Uthmān and 'Ali are different from Abū Bakr and Umar. What is the difference?

9. The father of Ja'far and 'Ali was different from them in one significant way. What was the difference?

10. When it comes to marriage, of the four daughters of the Prophet, Zainab was different from her other sisters. What is the specific difference?

11. Mention of shirts was made twice in sūrah Yūsuf. On both times the shirt was used to prove different things about Yūsuf. What were the differences?

12. Of all the battles between the Prophet and Quraish, the battle of Khandaq was different. The answer is not a ditch was dug. So, what is the answer?

13. The Prophet's marital life with Saudah was similar to the marital life with Khadījah in one way. But it was different from all other marriages that took place later in his life. What is the difference?

Before And After

1. He ruled before 'Uthmān, after Abū Bakr.

2. This sūrah, in her name, is placed before *Tā Hā* and after *Al-Kahf*.

3. He came before Prophet Muhammd and after Yahyā.

4. After this incident in Egypt, Mūsā fled to Madyan.

5. Ten brothers returned with this proof after dropping Yūsuf in the well.

6. The Israelites melted this metal to make something after Mūsā left for the mountain. What was the metal?

7. She received this before casting infant Māsā in the river.

8. After Khadījah's death, the Prophet married this woman to take care of his children.

9. She smiled saying "Old barren woman" after receiving this prophecy.

10. Before Āminah, Halīmah was Prophet's caretaker, after Āminah, he was Prophet's caretaker. Who was he?

11. Before a trade she was his employer, after the trade she was his wife. Who was she?

12. Before he wanted to kill his sister, after listening to *Tā Hā* he became a believer. Who was he?

13. After something was shown to Ya'qub he became convinced Yūsuf was alive. What was that?

14. Even after two of his sons accepted Islam, this renowned guardian did not accept Islam.

15. After she died, this would-be Khalīfa married her younger sister. Who was the elder sister who died?

16. Immediately before Ismā'īl and Ishāq there were two contemporary prophets, one was their father Ibrāhīm. Who was the other?

Juz Amma

1. How many sūrahs are includes in Juz Amma?

2. What is the first sūrah in the Juz Amma?

3. Which is the smallest sūrah in the Qur'ān in terms of number of verses and letters?

4. Which sūrah speaks of finding the Prophet as orphan, giving him shelter, guiding him and enriching him?

5. Which sūrah in Juz Amma refers to an event happened in the year the Prophet was born?

6. *Samad* is a Beautiful Name of Allah. In which sūrah you can find this name mentioned?

7. In a small sūrah in Juz Amma it says Shaitān whispers (*was-was*) in the hearts of man. By what name of Shaitan mentioned in that surah?

8. Which sūrah in Juz Amma can you find mention of galloping horses causing sparks of lights from the fiction of their hoof with rocks?

9. Which sūrah in Juz Amma speaks of angels descending with blessing until the time of Fajr?

10. Which sūrah in Juz Amma rebukes those people who neglect the orphans yet they do devotional salāt?

11. Which sūrah in Juz Amma speaks of human being would be like scattered moths at the time of Awakening?

12. Abū Lahab would burn in fire of flames, but his wife would have something around her neck. What is that?

13. A small sūrah in Juz Amma tells Hell would be *Hawiyah* and then explains the features of *Hawiyah* as a mother who nurses the child. Which is the sūrah?

14. Which sūrah in Juz Amma speaks about knowledge granted through use of pen?

15. Which sūrah in Juz Amma speaks about fig and olive in the background of Mount Sinai and Makkah?

16. The name Juz Amma is derived from the mention of *'Amma* in a sūrah. What is that sūrah?

Middle East Conflict

1. Yassir Arafat started a revolutionary party in Palestine. What is the name of that group?

2. Prior to his death, Yassir Arafat was confined in West Bank in a city. What was that city?

3. Yassir Arafat shared Noble Peace prize in the year 1994 with Yitzhak Rabin and another Israelite premier. What is his name?

4. A Palestinian guerilla group ambushed and killed 11 Israelite athletes in an Olympic Games in 1972. Where was the game held?

5. Under Ariel Sharon's command, 1000 innocent children were massacred in two refugee camps in 1982. What are the names of the twin camps?

6. The state of Israel was formed in 1948 through a declaration signed by the US and Britain. What is the name of the declaration?

7. In 1967 war between Israel and various Middle Eastern countries, Israel emerged victorious. It defeated Egypt, Syria and this country.

8. What accord was signed by Yitzhak Rabin and Yassir Arafat, meditated by Bill Clinton in the year 1993?

9. As a framework of peace initiatives in the Middle East, first Camp David Accord was signed in 1978 by Israel and an Arab nation. What was that nation?

10. An Arabic word about popular Palestinian uprising directed at ending Israelie occupation. The word came into common usage in English. What is the word?

11. In a landslide victory Ismail Haney and his party won the election in Palestine in 2006. Which party did he represent?

12. What is the name of the Israel's secret service intelligence operation?

13. Soon after Yassir Arafat died, who was elected PM/President of PLO?

14. Who was the prime minister of Israel when 1967 war between Israel and several Arab countries were fought?

15. What Palestinian guerrilla group was responsible for killing 11 athletes in 1972 Olympic games?

How Many

1. If you do all sunnat, fard and witr prayer (3) in a day, how many rak'at prayers would you have performed? (including *sunnat-i gharyil mu'akkadah* and *sunnat-i mu'akkadah*)

2. Other than the name of a sūrah, how many times the word "Muhammad" is mentioned in the Qur'ān

3. According to the Qur'ān how many years did Nūh live or his teachings lasted?

4. How many years did Abū Bakr rule as a *Khulafa-e-Rashidun*?

5. How many daughters of the Prophet were married to various Khalifas?

6. According to the Qur'ān how many nights of meditation was recommended for Mūsā?

7. Hudaibiya Treaty was singed to establish 10 years of peace, but how many years did it last?

8. Zakarriya was given a sign not to speak to people for certain number of days. How many days were mentioned in the Qur'ān?

9. If you make an intentional oath and break it, there are several options to expiate for it. The last option is to fast for certain day. How many days are prescribed?

10. How many months of Islamic calendar are considered to be sacred months?

11. In a solar year we have 365 days. How many days are in a lunar year?

12. How many of the Prophet's Companions received glad tidings of advance information about their admittance in the Heaven?

13. After the death of a husband how many days of Iddat a widow has to observe?

14. After divorce, how many days of statutory iddat a woman has to observe?

15. How many days of iddat should a divorced but pregnant woman observe?

16. How many years of married life did Prophet and Khadījah have together?

17. A particular night in the month of Ramadan is better than how many nights?

Legal Ruling

1. This term used to mean things that are permitted or lawful in Islam.

2. This term denotes something that is prohibited by Allāh and unlawful in Islam.

3. This term denotes something that is not expressly prohibited, but it is improper and unbecoming.

4. Only animal specifically mentioned in the Qur'ān whose meat is forbidden.

5. This drink is specifically forbidden in Islam.

6. Next to worshipping Allāh, this act is the second best activity.

7. In the Qur'ān this conduct is compared to eating flesh of dead brother.

8. The month when Hajj pilgrimage to Makkah can be undertaken.

9. Number of witness required in establishing a case of adultery.

10. How many female witnesses can be accepted in place of one male witness?

11. When a decision on family matter cannot be agreed upon, whose decision will ultimately be valid?

12. In this place hunting is prohibited.

13. What is the term for the duration of time allowed to a wife to remarry after divorce or after her husband dies.

14. What is the amount of inheritance share entitled for the adopted sons?

15. In Islam, open or hidden form of this conduct is forbidden.

16. The term indicates a fixed amount of money must be spent usually upon certain prescribed heads.

"Abū -"

1. This uncle Abū never accepted Islam yet cared for his nephew Muhammad (pbuh).

2. During Hijrat, this Abū accompanied Muhammad (pbuh).

3. This Abū is the nicknamed as Foremost among the Believers. Who was he?

4. When this person accepted Islam, the Prophet named him Abdur Rahman but he continued to be known by his name which means 'father of the kittens'.

5. Nicknamed "Father of Firebrands". His hands were condemned to perish.

6. This Abū was an arch enemy of Muhammad (pbuh) for a long time. He was married to famous woman named Hind.

7. Muhammad (pbuh) was briefly known by the name of his eldest son. What was the name he was known for?

8. His original name was Abdul Ka'bah. This Abū was popularly known as "As-Siddīq."

9. This notorious Abū was slain in Battle of Badr. Who was he?

10. This Abū is reported to be one of the ten Companions promised to enter the Paradise. He was son of Al-Jarrah. Who was he?

11. A city on the Persian Gulf, bordering Qatar, Oman and Saudi Arabia.

12. This Abū was instrumental in downfall of the Ummayad Caliphate and placing the Abbasid Caliphate in power.

13. This renowned Abū joined Yassir Arafat's guerilla group to promote violent opposition to Israel, and later was sentenced to death in absentia.

14. This Abū produced 4,800 Traditions of the Prophet, compiled in *Kitāb Al Sunnah.*

15. This Abū Al-Qāsim Mahmud Ibn -* , popularly known by this name. He is the author of a commentary of the Qur'ān titled *al-Kashshaf.*

16. When this Abū became head of the clan of Hāshim, he withdrew protection of Muhammad (pbuh).

17. In English he is known as Abulcasis, this Abū is considered as Islam's greatest medieval surgeon, whose medical texts influenced the European surgical procedures up until the Renaissance. What was his name?

Miscellaneous – I

1. Islam is symbolized by this tree. What is the tree?

2. The angel who stands guard on the Hell. Who is he?

3. When death comes, this angel will take the soul.

4. During the night of Mir'aj, Muhammad(pbuh) traveled from Masjid Al-Harām to this Masjid.

5. According to the Qur'ān the Jews say this person was the son of God.

6. Fir'awn asked Hāmān to build this so that he can see Allāh. What did he ask to be built?

7. Bitter and pungent tree that grows in the bottom of the Hell. What is the name of the tree?

8. The freedman and adopted son of the Prophet, later died in the battle of Mūtah.

9. This person is commonly known as the "Leader of the Hypocrites."

10. Tālūt undertook an expedition against this tyrant. Who was the tyrant?

11. This person spread a slander in the name of 'Ā'ishah.

12. Abd al-Uzza, a hostile uncle of the Prophet is more commonly known by this name.

13. Parts of sūrah Maryam was read out by Ja'far to this king.

14. In the Qur'ān, prophecy of birth of a son was sent to two women, one was Maryam, who was the other woman?

15. In the Qur'ān, prophecy of birth of a son was sent to two men, one was Ibrāhīm, who was the other man.

16. In the Qur'ān, the Israelites were compared with apes and swine for violating this ritual.

17. Hamzah was martyred in the Battle of Uhud by a spear thrown by a person. Who was the person that threw the spear?

18. After the Battle of Khandaq, Banu Qurayzah were adjudged war criminal for breaking treaty of neutrality. They opted for a judge to decide their case; a person they thought was their supporter. Who was the judge?

Miscellaneous – II

1. This golden animal used to produce bellowing sound when air blew through it. Which prophet's people made the animal to worship?

2. A person by this name was responsible for making the golden animal for worshipping.

3. In the story of the dwellers of cave, an animal is mentioned. What is that animal?

4. For how many days do the dwellers of cave thought they tarried in the cave?

5. Allāh knows how long the dwellers of cave tarried in the cave, but the Christians claim they tarried in the cave for total of this many year plus 9.

6. When Khidir and Mūsā set out together in their journey, what was the first strange thing Khidir did?

7. The four sacred months in Islam are Dhu al-Qadah, Dhu-al Hajj, Muharram and this month.

8. Allāh is not ashamed to strike a parable using anything as small as this insect.

9. What was the original name of Makkah, also mentioned in the Qur'ān?

10. The battle of Badr was partly stirred up when the Muslims intended to ambush a caravan of this person.

11. Iram is a place mentioned in the Qur'ān (89:7). Its people built columns, the like of which has not been built earlier. With which tribe the place was related?

12. To whom was "clothing of reverence" (*libās al-taqwā*) sent?

13. Other than being prophets, what is common about Yūnus, Nūh, Yūsuf, Luqmān and Muhammad(pbuh)?

14. Another name of Ka'bah which means "Sacred Sanctuary."

15. How long the 1967 war between Israel and Arab countries last?

16. Which wife of the Prophet gave him advice during the Treaty of Hūdaibiya?

Miscellaneous – III

1. Divine guests came to visit Ibrāhīm and this prophet.

2. Which is the most widely used 3 letter combination of abbreviations used in the Qur'ān?

3. During which prophet people hamstrung an animal to disobey Allāh?

4. Which prophet's community curved out exquisite dwellings on the rock?

5. The Prophet's two sons born of Khadījah died at early age. Who were they?

6. This prophet unintentionally killed a person and later ran away from administration for fear of death.

7. Who or what were *'asharah mubashsharah*?

8. Ancient Greeks thought the universe was created out of four elements, Earth, Air, Water and this substance.

9. One of the 99-names of Allāh. It means wise person, but also means a doctor of medicine. What is the name?

10. What is the general term for the revelation sent to the prophet Ibrāhīm?

11. This term indicates the practice of abstaining from food, drink, marital contact from dawn to dusk.

12. What was the name of the largest idol god in Ka'bah?

13. What is the name of the great-grandfather of the Prophet?

14. What is the name of the special supplication read in the witr prayer?

15. A rebel group was responsible for the assassination of 'Uthmān. What is the name of that group?

16. Dhu al-Qurnain filled up the space between the mountains with this element.

17. Before Muhammad (pbuh) was married to Khadījah, she sent him to Syria to do a trade on her behalf. She also sent a servant in the trade just to watch Muhammad (pbuh). Who was the servant?

Miscellaneous – IV

1. In this battle the strategic plan was to guard the wells. Which battle was that?

2. The first battle between the Muslims and the Quraish was fought in this month.

3. This declaration proclaimed Palestine as a "national home of the Jewish people."

4. Ja'far, the early convert and immigrant to Abyssinia had another brother who was an early convert too. Who was he?

5. It is said the 'Umar converted to Islam after hearing the recitation of a sūrah. What was that sūrah?

6. Prior to his death, Yassir Arafat was confined at this place, he was also buried here?

7. This person became chief of the clan of Hāshim after the former chief Abū Tālib died.

8. Out of the percent of spoils of war, what is the share of the Prophet?

9. This ancient trade route connected China with the West. What was its name?

10. In the history of Palestine in the year 2006 Ismail Hanieh created a sensation. What was that?

11. What was the name of a prison in Iraq that came to prominence during the US-Iraq war?

12. The teachings of this prophet particularly mention to keep correct balance and give proper measure.

13. In the year 1994 Yassir Arafat shared Nobel Peace Prize with two other leaders. Who were they?

14. 1962 Oscar winning movie narrates a true story about the Ottoman attempt to invade Hijāz, but the British destroyed the ploy. What is the name of the movie?

15. Moustapha Aqqad directed a two famous movies, one was "Muhammad", what was the other?

 Answers on page 122

The Last

1. Who was the last woman to be included as the wife of the Prophet?

2. He was the last of the four Rightly Guided Khalīfas. Who was his name?

3. In the order or revelation, the last complete sūrah to be revealed is included in the Juz Amma. Which is the sūrah to be revealed?

4. Although not the last sūrah to be revealed, what is the last sūrah in the Qur'ān?

5. The Prophet had many sons and daughters born to him. Who was the last daughter of the Prophet?

6. The Prophet had many sons and daughters born to him. Who was the last child of the Prophet born to him?

7. Which was the last major battle fought by the Prophet?

8. Which was the last major incident done by Khidir before he disclosed the reason for his surprising actions?

9. He was the last grandson of the Prophet. Who was he?

10. What were the last celestial object, the rising and setting of which lead Ibrāhīm question validity of worshipping these objects?

11. 'Abdul Muttalib had several daughters and sons born to him. Who was the last son of 'Abdul Muttalib?

12. Who was the last of the four Imams to form a Madhhab widely recognized among mainstream Muslims?

13. Who was the last of the Prophet's children to die?

14. When the Prophet passed away, he left behind many of his wives as widows. Who was the last of his wives to die?

15. In Shī'ite belief they have 12 Imams (*Ithna 'Asharīyah*). Who was the last of the 12 Imams?

16. During the mystic journey of Mi'rāj, what is the last place the Prophet reportedly went where nobody was allowed?

17. What was the last battle Hamza, the uncle of the Prophet, fought?

Answers to Quiz

The Prophet, His Family, His Life - I

1. At 40 years age
2. 23 years
3. Sunnah
4. Khadījah
5. Āmina
6. Cave Hira
7. Shepherd and trader
8. 63 years
9. 'Abd al-Muttalib (Prophet's grandfather)
10. Khadījah, wife of the Prophet. She was also the first person to accept Islam.
11. Hashim
12. Al-Qāsim
13. Zaynab, Ruqayya, Umm Kulthūm and Fātimah
14. 'Ā'ishah
15. 'Alī ibn Abī Tālib
16. Abū Tālib
17. Battle of Badr

The Prophet, His Family, His Life - II

1. 'Abdu Manāf. Grand father was 'Abd al-Muttalib, whose father was Hāshim. Hāshim's father was 'Abdu Manāf
2. Abū Tālib
3. His mother, Āmina
4. Birth of Muhammad
5. He was the father of the Prophet
6. Six children (Qāsim, Zaynab, Ruqayyah, Umm Kulthūm, Fātimah and a short-lived son named Ibrāhīm.
7. Fātimah
8. Uncle Abū Lahab
9. Death of the Prophet
10. Al-Amin
11. Migrated to Madinah
12. When he returned from cave Hira after receiving the first revelation.
13. Ten years
14. Cave of Thawr
15. Al-Isra
16. Halīmah

Names of Allāh

1. Ar-Rahmān
2. Ar-Rahīm
3. Al-Malik
4. Al-Khāliq
5. Al-Karīm
6. Al-Ghaffār
7. Al-Majīd
8. An-Nūr
9. The Praiseworthy
10. The Patient
11. The Unique
12. The Wise
13. The Just
14. The Source of Peace
15. The All Knowing
16. The Preserver

answers to beginners**Quiz**

Terminology - I

1. Adhān
2. Hadīth
3. Harām
4. Makrūh
5. Muqtadī
6. Mihrab
7. 'Umrah
8. Muhājirūn (sing. Muhājir)
9. Qiblah
10. Tawwaf
11. Rak'ah
12. Munāfiqūn (sing. Munāfiq)
13. Dhikr
14. Fatwā
15. Madrasah
16. I'tikāf
17. Tafsīr

Terminology - II

1. Ākhirah
2. Ansār
3. Janāzah
4. Fard
5. Qunūt
6. Sahūr
7. Sadaqah
8. Hāfiz
9. Tayammum
10. Sha'bān
11. Rūh
12. Nikāh
13. Muftī
14. Jizyah
15. Fiqh
16. 'Āshūrā'

Past Prophets - I

1. Hārūn
2. Yūnus, thrown into sea from a ship
3. Lūt
4. Jesus
5. Sulaimān
6. Dāwūd
7. Sālih
8. Zakariyyāh and Yahyā
9. Ismā'īl and Ishāq
10. Sulaimān
11. Mūsā
12. Hoopoe
13. 12 tribes
14. Hager (Hagirah)
15. Lūt
16. Yūsuf
17. Lūt

Past Prophets - II

1. Yūsuf	2. Mūsā
3. Ādam	4. Ibrāhīm
5. Mūsā	6. Ibrāhīm
7. 'Isā	8. Zakariyyāh
9. Yahyā	10. 'Isā
11. Sālih	12. Sulaimān
13. Ayyūb	14. Mūsa
15. Yūnus	

Qur'ān

1. Ramadan	2. 114 Surahs
3. 30 Juz	4. The Reading
5. 23 years	6. Angel Jibril
7. Cave Hira	8. 5 verses
9. Madīnah	10. Pen
11. Read	12. Baqarah
13. Tafsīr	14. Uthman

15. They are the translators of the Quran in English

16. Manzil	17. Zaid Ibn Thabit

18. Jibril

Sūrah

1. Al-Fīl	2. 3 Ayahs
3. Al-Qadr	4. Rukū'

5. Sūrah Lahab (after Abu Lahab) This sūrah is also known as Al-Masad

6. Fātiha	7. An-Nās
8. Al-Ikhlās	9. Maryam
10. An-Nahl (The Bee)	11. Sūrah #9, At-Ta'ubah
12. 114 times	13. Bārat
14. Al-Kahf	15. Sūrah Zilzal
16. Alif-Lām-Mīm	

17. Fātiha. The term in question means seven oft repeated.
18. Fātiha

Personality

1. Cassius Clay
2. 'Abd al-Muttalib
3. 'Umar al-Khattāb
4. Āsiyah
5. Khidir
6. Mutafa Kemal Ata Turk
7. Maurice Bucaille
8. Benazir Bhutto
9. Khālid ibn al-Walīd
10. Avicenna
11. Abu Hurairah
12. King Faisal
13. Akbar
14. Ghengis Khan
15. Kareem Abdul Jabbar
16. Hashim Rahman
17. Firdawsi

First

1. Bilal
2. Badr
3. Quba
4. Lailatul Qadr
5. Alī Ibn Abī Tālib
6. Abū Bakr
7. Al-Qasim
8. Zaynab
9. Al-'Alaq
10. Abyssinia or Ethiopia
11. 'Umar al-Khattāb
12. 8th of Dhu al-Hajj
13. Qabil or Cain (son of Adam)
14. Prince Salman Bandar
15. Dr. Abdus Salam in physics
16. Ta'if
17. Shirin Ebadi
18. Banu Qaynuka

"M" Word

1. Mu'adhdhin or Mu'azzin
2. Masiha
3. Minaret, Minbar is correct too
4. Mahdi
5. Mārūt
6. Mahr.
7. Mihrāb
8. Māliki school in the name of Mālik Ibn Anas
9. Maryam
10. Manna or Mann
11. Mikā'īl
12. Muhājir
13. Mi'rāj
14. Moon
15. Madyan
16. Munāfiq
17. Madyan

"S" Word

1. Sahabah	2. Safā
3. Sajdah	4. Shahīd
5. Shirk i.e. associating partners with Allāh	
6. Sīrah	7. Sheba
8. Sabbath	9. Salīh
10. Sodom or Sadūm	11. Shāf'ī
12. Salsabīl	13. Suhuf
14. Sharī'ah	15. Sha'bān
16. Safiullāh	17. Sāmirī or As-Sāmirī (20:87)
18. Shī'ah Muslims	

Fathers/Grandfathers

1. 'Abdullāh	2. Abū Bakr
3. 'Umar Ibn Al-Khattāb	4. Ya'qūb
5. Zakariyyāh	6. Dāwūd
7. Ibrāhīm	8. Azar
9. The Prophet Muhammad (pbuh)	10. 'Abd-al-Muttalib
11. 'Abd-al-Muttalib	
12. Abu Jahl (actual name was Abul Hakam)	
13. Abu Sufyān	14. Abū Tālib
15. Fātimah	16. Abū Hurairah

Miscellaneous - I

1. Dhul-Hajj	2. Muharram
3. Dhul-Hajj	4. Hamzah
5. Juz Amma	6. Ibrāhīm
7. Euphratis	8. Muslim
9. Jibril	10. Alī Ibn Abī Tālib
11. Eleven stars and the sun and the moon	12. Indonesia
13. Alchemy	14. Towards Jerusalem
15. Aqiqah	16. Bakkah
17. Halīmah	18. Bilāl Ibn Ribah

Miscellaneous - II

1. 25 years
2. 63 years of age
3. Yathrib
4. Makkah, when they are around the Ka'bah
5. The Quraish
6. Āyah
7. Abū Bakr
8. Ottoman Empire
9. Mariah
10. Abrahah
11. Alī Ibn Abī Tālib
12. Mount Sinai, Tuwā is acceptable
13. Bukhāri
14. Ibrāhīm
15. Ahlul Kitāb
16. Gog and Magog or Ya'jūj and Ma'jūj
17. Umayyad Dynasty

Miscellaneous - III

1. They are four books of authentic Hadīth
2. Abū Bakr
3. The last Hajj performed by the Prophet
4. Paradise
5. An-Nasr
6. Abū Bakr
7. When first 5 verses of Al-'Alaq were revealed
8. 2 times, in two rakat of the prayer
9. 7 verses, most frequently recited sūrah is Fātihah
10. Fasting during the month of Ramadan, see 2:183
11. Zaid ibn Thabit
12. 632 C.E.
13. Uthman ibn Affan
14. Role of Hamzah, the uncle of the Prophet,
15. Saudi Arabia
16. Mustafa Kemal, the first president of Republic of Turkey. He modernized Turkey.
17. Avicenna or Ibn Sina

answers to advanced**Quiz**

"A" Word

1. Awakening
2. Abyssinia
3. Abrahah
4. Asr
5. Arafat
6. Ashura
7. Aqabah
8. Arkan al-Islam
9. Asma al Husna
10. Alhambra mosque
11. Abū Dāwūd
12. 'Ā diyā
13. Alexander the Great
14. Āsiyah, wife of Pharaoh
15. 'Ankabūt
16. 'Alaq
17. 'Ādiyāt
18. Ādam (7:23)

"B" Word

1. Bebel or Babylon
2. Byzantine
3. Banlges / Bracelets
4. Binyamin
5. Bedouins
6. Bayyinah
7. Bilāl ibn Rabah
8. Birds (tāir)
9. Bahira
10. Barzakh
11. Bāligh
12. Baitu'l Ma'mūr
13. Bid'ah
14. Bukhāri
15. Bātin
16. Barnabas
17. Baitu-l Māl

"C" Word

1. Copper
2. Coptic
3. Cannan
4. Camel
5. CAIR
6. Crusade
7. Constantinople
8. Camp David Accord
9. Camel
10. Crescent
11. Compulsion
12. Cave
13. Carrion (dead animal)
14. Concubine
15. Clergy
16. Cattle

"D" Word

1. Dajjāl
2. Damascus
3. Duldul
4. Dāwūd
5. Deeds
6. Dirham
7. Druz
8. Debt
9. Day of Judgment (as mentioned in sūrah #82)
10. Da'wah
11. Dārus Salām
12. Darvesh
13. Deluge
14. Devil
15. Dower

"G" Word

1. Gold
2. Gambling
3. Ghazu
4. Al-Ghāsiyah
5. Ginger
6. Ghulām
7. Goliath , mentioned in 2:251, where he is mentioned as Jālūt
8. Gomorrah
9. Gossip
10. Gospel, this term applies to the whole of the New Testament
11. Al-Ghayb
12. Ghatafān or Ghifār – any answer is acceptable
13. Genesis
14. Garden
15. Golden calf
16. Galilee

"H" Word - I

1. Hijra
2. Hajj
3. Hager or Hājirah
4. Hārūn
5. Hafsah
6. Hashr
7. Hūd
8. Hūdaibiyah
9. Hajr Aswad
10. Hubal
11. Hamzah
12. Habīl
13. Hawwariyyun
14. Heart (40:18)
15. Hāmān
16. Hūrūn (20:94)

"H" Word – II

1. Halīmah	2. Hypocrites
3. Hunting, Haraba (war)	4. Humazah
5. Hamas	6. Hazrat
7. Hizbullah	8. Hadith Qudsi

9. "Hidden Imam", he is otherwise known as Mahdi

10. Hadramauth	11. Hadīd
12. Hāfiz	13. Hā Mīm

14. Hirā mountain where the Prophet received first revelation

15. Horses (38:32-33)	16. Hunain

"K" Word

1. Ka'bah	2. Kāfir
3. Kabīrah	4. Kalimah
5. Kafan	6. Kāhin
7. Karbalā	8. Kiswah
9. Kinanah	10. Kisrā
11. Khutbah	12. Khul
13. Khidir	14. Khazraj
15. Kharāj	16. Khaibar

"M" Word

1. Manāt	2. Muhaddis
3. Muharram	4. Mujāhidun
5. Maut	6. Mahram
7. Mīqat	8. Muslim League
9. Mujtahid	10. Mu'tazilites
11. Millah	12. Mamlūk
13. Miskīn	14. Majūs or Magians (22:17)
15. Miswāk	16. Mūsāllā

"Q" Word

1. Qābīl	2. Al-Qāsim
3. Qiblah	
4. Qubā – a place 3 miles from Madīnah	5. Qarun
6. Al-Qāri‘ah	7. Qārī
8. Dhu al – Qurnain	9. Quraish
10. Qur'ān (59:21)	11. Qamr (the Moon)
12. Qalm (the Pen)	13. Qiyamah
14. Quraish (see sūrah. 106).	15. Qiyās
16. Qiblah (2:145)	

"T" Word

1. Tabūk	2. Tābi‘ūn
3. Tā'if	4. Tāghūt
5. Tā Hā	6. Takbīr
7. Talmud	8. Tamīm
9. Tafsīr	10. Talhah
11. Taqlīd	12. Taubah
13. Tuwā	14. Tilāwat
15. Tasnīm	16. Tālūt

Earlier Prophets-I

1. Shu‘aib, (Mūsā's father in law. He is mentioned as Jethro. Some think Jethro was not Shu‘aib)

2. Yūnus, cast into sea after draw of lots	3. Yūsuf
4. Tūr, Sinai, Tuwā – all answers are OK	5. Mūsā
6. Yūsuf	7. Luqmān
8. North of Hijāz, close to present day Sinai	
9. Lūt	10. Nūh's son
11. Sālih	12. Hūd
13. Yahyā, (John, the Baptist)	14. Shu‘aib
15. Luqmān	16. Dāwūd

Earlier Prophets-II

1. Sulaimān
2. Cows
3. Mūsā
4. People of Hūd, the 'Ād.
5. Ibrāhīm
6. Gog and Magog or Ya'jūj and Ma'jūj
7. Fish (18:61-63)
8. Fear of capital punishment for inadvertently killing an Egyptian
9. A wolf
10. Junction of two sea
11. Shu'aib
12. Sulaimān
13. Mūsā
14. Dāwūd (see 21:78-79)
15. Ibrāhīm
16. Yūnus, due to a fish saving his life.

Former Prophets - Trivia

1. Sulaimān (27:19)
2. Dāwūd (38:22-24)
3. 'Isā (3:59).
4. Sulaimān (27:39)
5. Ayyūb (38:41), remember, interpretation of the verse varies.
6. Nūh when he was building ark on dry land (11:38)
7. Sulaimān (38:33)
8. Zakariyyāh (19:11)
9. Ismā'īl (37:102)
10. Ibrāhīm (19:46-47)
11. Yahyā (19:13-14)
12. 'Isā (19:16)
13. Zakariyyāh, prayed to have a child born to him (19:4-6)
14. 'Isā (19:26)
15. Mūsā (28:24).

Prophet Muhammad (s)-I

1. Banu Hāshim
2. 11 A.H.
3. Al-Āmīn
4. 26 years
5. Ahmad
6. Religion of Ibrāhīm
7. Year of Sadness
8. Bahīra, the Monk
9. 40 thousand
10. Mi'rāj
11. He was father of the Prophet.
12. 1st wife of the Prophet, Khadījah
13. Zainab bint Khuzaimah
14. Zaynab
15. Ibrāhīm
16. Waraqah

Prophet Muhammad (s)-II

1. 'Abdullah ibn Surayh. He was also known as Ibn Umm Maktūm
2. Sūrah 'Abasa   3. 13 women
4. At-Taubah or Al-Bara'at   5. An-Nasr (#110)
6. Salmān the Persian   7. Saudah
8. Brothers and sister (children of the Prophet) Al-Qāsim was the Prophet's first child, he died as a toddler, and Al-Tāhir died soon after his birth.
9. Maymūnah   10. Battle of Uhud
11. Honey   12. Soothsayer who uttered rhymes
13. South. Mt. Hirā' is located south of Makkah
14. 'Umar and his daughter Hafsah   15. He dug a ditch around Madīnah
16. Najrān

The Qur'ān

1. 6237 or 6236 based on where a verse is broken.
2. Six sūrahs, #2, 3, 29, 30, 31 and 32   3. Various names of the Qur'ān
4. Recitation of the Qur'ān   5. 27th night
6. 14 different alphabets   7. 29 Sūrahs
8. As-Shura (#42)   9. 'Uthmān
10. Vowel (tashkeel) marks added to facilitate easy reading.
11. Sūrah Baqarah v. 255   12. Yā Sīn
13. Tawrat (the Scripture of Mūsā, 2:53; 21:48)
14. Zaid bin Thābit   15. Tā'if (43:32)
16. 15 verses. Fourteen places of prostration in the Quran as agreed upon by Muslim religious scholars and Ulama, while Imam Shafi'i suggests prostration at Verse 77of Sūrah 22 Al-Hajj

The Qur'ān Trivia

1. 558 rukū's   2. 86 Makkan sūrahs
3. 28 Madīnan sūrahs   4. Letter 'ain (ع)
5. Sūrah 61, verse 6   6. Jinn
7. In the holy book of the Sikh, called Granth Sahib
8. 43 A.H. or 665 C.E.   9. Muhkam and mutashābih (3: 7)
10. 22 years, 5 months 14 days
11. Fatrah – some say it lasted as long as 2 years and 6 months, but opinion differs
12. Popularly believed to be 99. Total different names are 105. Names like Al-Mun'imu, Al-Rabb, Al-Sadiq, Al-Sattar are surprisingly not included in the list of 99 names.

13. 'Azīz, mentioned twice in v 30 and 51. Some say 'Azīz is not a proper name, but designation of the person.
14. The Prophet Muhammad (33:40)   15. 'Uthman ibn 'Affān
16. 7:206 – the very last verse of sūrah Al-A'rāf
17. In sūrah Al-Ahzab, 33:56   18. In sūrah Mā'idah, 5:3

Battle

1. Battle of Uhud   2. Battle of Badr
3. Battle of Uhud   4. Battle of Badr
5. Battle of Badr (in battle of Khandaq sand storm caused havoc to the enemy)
6. Expedition of Tabūk   7. Battle of Badr
8. Battle of Badr (8:9)   9. Battle of Uhud (3:124)
10. Battle of Khaybar   11. Battle of Hunain
12. Ahzāb or Battle or Trenches   13. Battle of Hunain
14. To dig a trench or ditch in the battle of al-Khandaq
15. Abū Jahl   16. 1/5th part or 20% (8:41)

Companions

1. Alī Ibn Abū Tālib   2. Alī Ibn Abū Tālib
3. Bilāl   4. "Uthmān Ibn 'Affān
5. Ja'far ibn Abū Tālib   6. 'Umar Ibn al-Khattāb
7. Abdullah Ibn Jubayr   8. Muawiyah Ibn Abū Sufyān
9. Alī Ibn Abū Tālib   10. Zaid Ibn al-Hārith
11. Al-Khattāb   12. 'Abd Allāh Ibn al-'Abbās
13. "Uthmān Ibn 'Affān   14. Khālid ibn al-Walīd
15. "Uthmān Ibn 'Affān   16. Salmān al-Fārsi

The Hereafter

1. Seven   2. Pitch or tar
3. Zaqqūm   4. Iron (22:21)
5.Banana   6. Silk
7. Camphor   8. Musk (83:26)
9. Salsabīl   10. Salām
11. Mālik   12. To their back (84:10)
13. Pearl (52:24)   14. Pearl
15. Jesus   16. Carpet

Sūrah – I

1. Muqatta'āt or Al-Fawatih
2. An-Nasr, Al-Kauthar, Al-'Asr. Al Kauthar is the smallest.
3. Al-Kahf
4. Ar-Rūm
5. Yūnus
6. Mā'idah
7. At-Taubah
8. Bani Isrā'īl or Al-Isra (# 17)
9. An-Nās
10. Al-Lahab or Masad
11. Al- Mā'ūn
12. Al-'Asr
13. Al-Qadr
14. At-Tīn
15. Al-Zalzalah
16. Al-Qāri'ah

Sūrah – II

1. At-Takāthur
2. Al-Fīl
3. Al-'Asr
4. At-Tīn (The Fig)
5. Al-Hadīd (the Iron) & Al-Zukhrūf (The Gold)
6. Sād (# 38), Qāf (# 50)
7. Al-Qalam (the Pen)
8. Ar-Rūm (The Romans)
9. Al Fīl (The Elephant)
10. An-Nūr (24:2)
11. Seven, sūrah 40 through sūrah 46
12. Ar-Rūm
13. Al-Jāthiyah (# 45)
14. As-Sajdah (# 32)
15. Al-Falaq (#113), sūrah # 89 Al-Fajr is incorrect answer, as the timing of Fajr is well before daybreak.
16. Sūrah Baqarah – it has 286 verses
17. Sūrah Baqarah, verses 184 and 185

First Verse of a Sūrah

1. Al-Kāfirūn #109
2. Al-Mā'un #107
3. Al-Qadr #97
4. 'Abasa #80
5. At-Tīn # 95
6. Al-A'la #87
7. Al-Burūj #85
8. Al-Anfāl #8
9. Al-Muddaththir #74
10. At-Taubah or Al-Bara'at #9
11. Bani- Isrā'īl or Al-Isra #17
12. Al-Qamar #54
13. Al-Mujādilah #58
14. Nūh #71
15. Al- Jinn #72
16. Maryam #19 [the only Sūrah to start with 5-letter combination. Sūrah 42 also has 5 letter combination, but they are placed in two separate verses]
17. Alif Lām Mīm
18. Alam tara kaifa fa'ala rabbuka biashāb al-fīl, (Sūrah al-Fīl).

"Ibn-"

1. Ibn Sīnā
2. Muhammad (pbuh)
3. Ibn Mājah
4. Ibn Battuta
5. Ibn Kathīr
6. Ahmad Ibn Hanbal
7. Husain
8. Ibn 'Abbās ('AbdAllāh Ibn al-'Abbās
9. Muwaiyyah
10. Mālik Ibn Anas
11. Ibn Majīd
12. Ibn Hazam
13. Ibn Khaldūn (Abd Al-Rahman)
14. Ibn Taymiyah
15. Ibn Ishāq
16. Ibn al-'Arabi

Exegetes, Exegesis

1. Abd Allāh Ibn Al-'Abbās
2. Tafsīr bir-ray
3. George Sale
4. Tafsīr al-Tabari
5. Al-Zamakhsharī
6. Al-Husain Al-Razi
7. 'Umar al-Baidawī
8. Tahfimul Qur'ān
9. Tafsīr Ibn-Kathīr
10. Fi Zilal al-Qur'ān
11. At-Tabari
12. Muhammad Rashid Rida
13. Tafsīr bil-ishara
14. Jalal al-Deen al-Suyūtī
15. Mu'tazila
16. Ignáz Goldziher

Dynasty

1. Ummayad
2. Pahlavi
3. Fatimid Dynasty
4. Ayyubid Dynasty
5. Ummayad
6. Fatimid Dynasty
7. Mongols
8. Abd ar-Rahman III
9. Buyids (also known as Buwayids)
10. Seljuks
11. Mamluk Dynasty
12. Seljuks
13. Mughals
14. Safavid Dyansty
15. Ghaznavids
16. Jalaluddin Rumi

Terminology – I

1. Bida'at
2. Jizyah
3. Madhab
4. Ijmā
5. Rashīdun
6. Tawāf
7. Hawwariyyun
8. Fitnah
9. Ijtihād
10. 'Umrah
11. Tahajjud
12. Tauhīd
13. Jāhilliyyah
14. Talbbīyah
15. Ghazu
16. Dhimmi

Terminology – II

1. Fatwā
2. Dhikr
3. Tābi'ūn
4. Tajweed
5. Isnad
6. Iqāmah
7. Talmud
8. Sirah
9. 'Aqīqah
10. Burqa'
11. Daif
12. Ijaz
13. Intifada
14. Matn
15. Taqlīd
16. 'Urs
17. Fard Kifā'ī

Terminology – III

1. Paigambar
2. Rahīl or Rehal
3. 'Ulamā
4. Wakīl
5. Walīmah
6. Wazīfah
7. Zabīhah
8. Sahāba
9. Zarrah (99:7-8)
10. Witr
11. Salsbīl (76:18-19)
12. Iqāmah
13. Lauhu Mahfūz (85:22)
14. Niyah
15. Nisāb
16. Li'ān
17. Mut'ah marriage

Cities, Countries

1. Hijāz
2. Najrān
3. Byzantine or The Romans
4. Qatar
5. Iran
6. Iraq
7. Egypt
8. Yemen
9. Sumatra
10. Brunei
11. Pakistan
12. Kyrgyzstan
13. Tunisia
14. Persia or present day Iran. Salmān the Persian came from this country.
15. Abyssinia. Ja'far lead first Muslim refugees to Abyssinia to emperor Negus
16. Damascus

Clue Words - I

1. Mūsā was placed in a basket that was cast into river and his sister walked by the river side (20:39)
2. Nūh and the Great Deluge
3. Yūsuf – he was dropped in a well by the brothers, he dreamt about his prominence and ruled Egypt
4. Mūsā was appointed 40 nights of devotion in a mountain (2:51; 7:142).
5. Sālih and his camel, people hamstrung the camel.
6. Mūsā sensed fire in a mountain, walked to it and received revelation (20:10; 27:7; 28:29)
7. Guests of Ibrāhīm, he brought out roasted food and the messengers made a prophecy of birth of his son (11:69; 15:51-52; 51:24-25).
8. Lut to his people
9. Mūsā and his staff, the rod was cast, it turned into serpent and swallowed other serpents (7:107-108; 20:17-23)
10. Ādam discovered his shame upon approaching the tree and then tried to cover himself (7:20-22).
11. Sulaimān and the throne in Sheba (27:38-42).
12. Dhu al-Qurnain and his dealing with Ya'jūj-Ma'jūj (18:94-98).
13. Hajirah (Hager) running for water when infant Ismā'īl was born
14. Cave where the Prophet and Abū Bakr hid during their Hijrah and a spider made a cobweb at the entrance
15. Signing of Treaty of Hūdaibiyah. Pilgrimage was intended, but ended up without pilgrimage after negotiation with the Quraish.
16. Dāwūd and his use of Iron – he made coats of mail with iron (34:10-11).

Clue Words - II

1. Hajj – chanting of Labbayek is done during Hajj, Aswad refers to the black stone in Ka'bah, Arafah is the place of congregation.
2. Mūsā was involved in a brawl between and Egyptian and an Israelites and in the process of solving the brawl he hit the Egyptian, killing him instantly.
3. Incidents at the time of Hijrat, the Prophet hid in the cave Thaur, spider spun a web in front of the cave, and at Quba the Prophet built first mosque for Muslims.
4. Mūsā receiving revelation after seeing fire in the mountain (20:10-14).
5. Reference of Dāwūd, mountains praised with him (21:79) and he melted iron (34:10-11).
6. Prisoners with Yūsuf and their dream about bird and bread (12:36,41).
7. Yūnus abandoned his community, boarded a ship and the sailors thought he brought evil omen
8. Mūsā helped women near the well (28:23-24).
9. During mystic travel in search of knowledge, Mūsā told his servant to bring breakfast, they carried a fish with them (18:62-63).
10. Maryam moved to an eastern place during her pregnancy (19:16, 23-26).
11. The Prophet turned away from a blind person, mentioned in sūrah 'Abasa.
12. Yūsuf's brother was accused of stealing King's cup in his sack.
13. Elephant army of Abrahah came to ravage Ka'bah.
14. Lailatul Qadr, a night of which is better than thousand months, angels descend on the night
15. Abū Lahab was cursed to perish in sūrah Lahab.
16. Hudaibiya Treaty. It was intended for pilgrimage, but ended up being cancelled pilgrimage but turned out to be a clear victory.

Who Said - I

1. Shaitān (7:12)
2. Sulaimān (27:20)
3. Ibrāhīm (37:102)
4. Maryam (19:20)
5. Mūsā (20:180
6. Zakariyyāh (19: 8)
7. Yūsuf (12:93)
8. Fir'awn (28:38)
9. Mūsā (28:33)
10. 'Isā (5:114)
11. Ibrāhīm (19:42)
12. Yūsuf
13. Iblīs
14. Sulaimān (27:44)
15. Fir'awn (20:71)
16. Brothers of Yūsuf

Who Said - II

1. Lūt
2. Mūsā
3. Maryam's mother
4. Khidir (18:75)
5. Hārūn
6. Fir'awn (10:90)
7. Nūh (11:38)
8. Shu'aib (11:84)
9. Aziz, the Egyptian (12:21)
10. Ibrāhīm (14:37)
11. Nūh's son (11:43)
12. The dwellers of cave (18:19)
13. Dhu al-Qurnain (18:96)
14. Mūsā (26:21)
15. Bilqīs, Queen of Sheba (27:29)
16. Luqmān (31:13)
17. Nūh, cried to Allāh for safety of his son (11:45)

Who Said – III

1. Maryam
2. 'Isā
3. Ya'qūb
4. Shaitān
5. Sulaimān
6. Khidir (18:67)
7. Habīl or Abel
8. Bilqīs, Queen of Sheba (27:32)
9. The Jews (2:142)
10. Tālūt (2:249)
11. Bilqīs (27:44)
12. Angels (2:32)
13. Ibrāhīm (2:258) – as he challenged Nimrod
14. A person from the caravan, after picking up Yūsuf from the well
15. One of the prisoner with Yūsuf (12:36)   16. Zakariyyāh
17. A witness [or a servant] in Yūsuf's house (12:26-27)

Places in the Qur'ān

1. Yathrib
2. Jerusalem
3. Abyssinia
4. City of Ta'if
5. Madyan
6. Egypt
7. Madīnah
8. Badr
9. Uhud
10. Aqabah
11. Judi (11:44)
12. Tabūk
13. Najrān
14. Black Sea (18:86)
15. Ela (7:163)
16. Jerusalem (17:4)
17. 80 miles

Islamic History – I

1. 8 years in 8A.H.
2. Sir Muhammad Iqbal
3. Abūl Ala Mawdudi
4. Harun al-Rashid
5. Aurangzeb
6. Yahyā, (John the Baptist)
7. Rashid Rida
8. Ghazzali (Abū Hamid Muhammad)
9. Syyid Qutb
10. Abū Sufyān
11. Al-Khwarizmi
12. The death of Khadījah and uncle Abū Tālib
13. 624 A.H., the verse was 2:142
14. 1924
15. Tariq Ibn Ziyad
16. Abbasid

Islamic History – II

1. Harun al-Rashid
2. 'Ali ibn Abū Tālib
3. Umar al-Khattāb
4. Sūrah Maryam
5. Ma'mun al-Rashid
6. Abbasid
7. Umm al-Fadl
8. Ten years
9. Suhayl b. 'Amar
10. Mughal Empire in India
11. Muhammad bin Qasim
12. Sher Shah Suri
13. 'Ā'ishah
14. Afghanistan
15. Shah Jahan
16. India

Communities, Nations, Tribes, Emperors

1. Banu Hāshim
2. Nasārā
3. Banu Qaynuqah
4. Aws and Khazraj
5. Banu Qaynuqah
6. 12 tribes
7. Quraish
8. Ād
9. Banu Qurayzah
10. Babylon
11. Sheba or Saba
12. Egypt
13. Heraclius
14. Dhul Qurnain
15. Khushro
16. Nimord

Wives of the Prophet

1. Khadījah
2. 'Ā'ishah
3. Khadījah
4. Hafsah
5. Zainab bint Jash
6. Maimūnah
7. Sawdah
8. Umm Salama
9. 26 years, (25 years according to some commentators)
10. Between the age of 55 and 60 years of age
11. Zainab (bint Jash) Zainab (bint Khuzayma)
12. Juwayrīyah bint Al-Harith
13. Umm Habībah
14. Safīya bint Huyayy
15. Maimūnah bint al-Harith
16. Hafsah

Hajj

1. 7 times
2. Muzdalifa
3. Ihrām
4. Arafāt
5. 'Ali Ibn Abi Tālib
6. Jamrah - Aqubah, Wusta and Sughra
7. Mīqat
8. Sayi
9. Eid ul-Adhā
10. Muzdalifa
11. Throw 7 pebbles
12. Wuqūf
13. Kiswah
14. Hajar al-Aswad
15. Talbīyah
16. Valley of Arafāt
17. During tawaf of Ka'bah
18. Pelt stones at them, they are the three symbols of Shaitān

Number

1. 9 Signs
2. 7 verses
3. 12 months
4. 313 Muslims
5. 10,000 Muslims
6. 86 (28 in Madīnah)
7. 29 sūrahs
8. 29 years
9. 227 verses
10. 1,400
11. One, Fātimah
12. 4 Gospels
13. 12 sons (Yūsuf, Binyamin and 10 step brothers)
14. 70 Muslims.
15. 28 years
16. 3 years
17. Six times (S. 2, S. 3, S.29, S. 30, S. 31 and S. 32).
18. 14 letters

Year

1. 1776 C.E.	2. 622 C.E.
3. 624 C.E.	4. 570 C.E.
5. 628 C.E.	6. 50,000 years
7. 1967	8. 1948

9. 1993
10. 545 C.E. 'Abdullāh was 25 years when he died, thus, approx. 570-25=545
11. 580 C.E.
12. 615 C.E., followed by another team in 616 C.E.

13. 621 C.E.	14. 625 C.E.

15. 632 C.E. the year the Prophet passes away   16. 70 C.E.

Authors

1. Muhammad Asad	2. Jeffrey Lang
3. Maurice Bucaille	4. Syed Qutb
5. Muhammad Asad	6. Omar Khayyam
7. Sayeed Ruhollah Khomeini	8. Karen Armstrong
9. Martin Ling (Abū Bakr Siraj Al Din)	10. Michael H. Hart
11. Paul Findley	12. Suyuti
13. Ibn Khaldun	14. Muhammad Rashid Rida
15. Bukhari	16. Ibn Sina
17. Firdawsi	

Names of Allāh

1. 99, (although the total is many more than that)

2. Al-Latīf	3. Al-Muqīt
4. Al-Haiy	5. Al-Wālī
6. Al-Hādī	7. Al-Hasīb
8. As-Shahid	9. The Loving
10. The Great One	11. The Aware
12. The Provider	13. The Holy
14. The Opener	15. The Great One
16. The First	

Personality

1. Muhammad 'Ali Jinnah
3. Sir Muhammad Iqbal
5. Harun Al-Rashid
7. Lawrence of Arabia (T. E. Lawrence)
9. Yazīd-I
11. Al-Ghazzali
13. 'Ā'ishah
15. Hasan Al-Banna
2. Shah Wali Ullah
4. Malcom X
6. Egypt
8. Jalal ad-Din Rūmi
10. Ibn Khaldun
12. Muhammad ibn al-Wahhab
14. Ghengis Khan
16. Ibn Khaldun

Contemporary Muslim Personalities

1. Jeffrey Lang
3. Mahatir Mohammad
5. Abdul Karim al-Jabbar
7. Hakeem Olajuwon
9. Murad Hoffman
11. Ismail Haniya
13. Shirin Ebadi
15. Nasser Hussain
16. Muhammad Yunus and Gramin Bank
2. Yusuf al-Qaradawi
4. Hashim Rahman
6. Kareem Abdul Jabbar
8. Cat Stevens
10. Amina Wadood
12. Mahmood Abbas
14. Naguib Mahfouz

Khalīfa, Caliphate

1. 'Ali Ibn Abū Tālib
3. Iraq
5. Baghdad
7. Yazīd – I
9. 29 years
11. Damascus
13. Mongols
15. Abbasids
17. Mamluk
2. The Thousand and One Night
4. Damascus
6. Mu'āwiyah –I
8. Mu'āwiyah -I
10. Hasan
12. Al-Mansur
14. Abd Ar-Rahman III
16. Imāms

The Only

1. Abū Bakr
2. Māriyah
3. Ibrāhīm
4. Inside the Ka'bah
5. Maryam
6. Mūsā
7. As-Shura (# 42)
8. 'Umar ibn Al-Khattāb
9. Ar-Rūm (The Romans)
10. 'Abasa
11. Zaid ibn Haritha
12. An-Naml (in the beginning and in v. #30).
13. Al-Lahab, the uncle of the Prophet (Sūrah # 111)
14. During Isrā
15. Dāwūd
16. Sād (# 38)
17. 'Ali Ibn Abu Tālib

Shī'ite Islam

1. Hasan, son of 'Ali
2. 'Ali ibn Abū Tālib
3. Mu'āwiyah
4. Rebellion against Mu'āwiyah by Hussain.
5. Karbala
6. The Twelvers (Ithna 'Ashariyah)
7. Muhammad al Muntazar
8. Hidden Imam
9. The Hidden Imam, the 12th Imam
10. Ismā'īlis
11. Ismā'īl (son of Ja'far as-Sadiq).
12. Imam
13. Muharram
14. Fātimid dynasty
15. Druz

Denominations & Sects

1. Successor
2. Fātimids
3. Zaydism
4. Kharijism
5. Nusayris
6. Druz
7. Bahai
8. Ahmadiyya Qadiani
9. Lost-Found Nations of Islam
10. Druz
11. Mirza Ghulam Ahmad – claimed to be a prophet.
12. Bahai
13. Warith Deen Muhammad
14. Malcom X

Crime and Punishment

1. He was killed in the battle
2. Men were killed, the women and children were made prisoners (33:26-27)
3. Death penalty   4. He was detained in Egypt
5. 9 years   6. Nothing, He forgave them (9:43)
7. Their homes were turned upside down (11:82)
8. Burn in pyre of fire (21:68)
9. Cut their legs in opposite direction and crucify them (20:71)
10. 100 stripes (24:2). Death penalty is not mentioned in the Qur'ān
11. 4 witness (24:4,13)
12. Seek death upon them for lying (3:61)   13. Expelled from Madīnah (59:2)
14. Paying blood money
15. No punishment, not death (2:217, 3:90; 5:54; 16:106)
16. Chopping off hands (5:38)

Title

1. Jibril   2. As-Siddīq
3. Ummu'l Kitāb
4. Makkah, *Ummu'l Qura* means mother of cities,
5. Ibrāhīm   6. Khālid Ibn Walīd
7. Wives of the Prophet
8. Abū Hurairah (literal meaning of his name),
9. Camel   10. Garland
11. Al-Furqān   12. 'Abdul-Uzza
13. Mūsā
14. Abū al-Hakam aka Amar ibn Hishām
15. Yūnus, the title means companion of fish.   16. 'Isā
17. Wazir or Vizir

Parables

1. Spider (29:41)   2. Mosquito or gnat (2:26)
3. Seven (2:261)   4. One hundred (2:261)
5. Dew (2:265)   6. Smooth rock (2:264)
7. Mirage (24:39)   8. Ash (14:18)
9. Donkey carrying a load (62:5)   10. Dog (7:176)
11. Lamp and light stand (24:35)   12. Qur'ān (59:21)
13. It gets uprooted (14:26)   14. Vineyard (18:32)
15. Edge of a collapsing bank (9:109) 16. Thread (16:92)

Brothers, Sisters

1. Hārūn (20:94)
2. Cain or Qābīl (5:27-31)
3. Maryam
4. 'Ā'ishah
5. Binyamin/Bejamin
6. Ten
7. Abdullah, prophet's father
8. Abū Lahab
9. Ruqaiyah, and Umm Kulthūm
10. Ismā'īl
11. Habil and Qābīl – sons of Ādam
12. Hamzah
13. 'Ali ibn Abi Tālib
14. Zainab bint Jahsh
15. Zainab bint Khuzaymah
16. None, he was the only child of his parents.

Father and Forefather

1. Āzar
2. 'Adb al Muttalib
3. Dāwūd
4. Zakariyyāh
5. Ishāq
6. 'Abd Al Muttalib
7. Ibrāhīm
8. Ja'far
9. Ibn 'Abbās
10. 'Abdullāh
11. Yūsuf
12. Luqmān
13. Muhammad (pbuh)
14. Zayd
15. Ismā'īl
16. Abū Sufyān
17. Son of Nūh

Common

1. They wrote biographies of the Prophet
2. They translated the Quran in English
3. They are compilers of Hadīth
4. They were female goddesses in Kabah
5. They are all angels
6. They are all brothers, son of 'Abdul Muttalib
7. They bore children of the Prophet
8. They were Ummayad Caliphs
9. They are various names of the Qur'ān
10. They were assassinated, but Abū Bakr was not,
11. They are son-in-law of the Prophet
12. The Prophet married their daughter(s)
13. These are various names of Hell.
14. They are various names of the Qur'ān
15. They were scribes of the Qur'ān
16. These are some of the signs shown by Mūsā
17. Seven Imams are common among all denominations, majority Shī'ahs beleive in 12 Imams, the Seveners believe only in first 7 Imams.

The Qur'ān and the Bible

1. Sulaimān

2. Yayhā or John the Baptist

3. Ya'qūb on Yūsuf's dream

4. Eve

5. Jealous

6. Wife of Lūt

7. Ismā'īl

8. Zakariyyāh

9. Ibrāhīm (he did not abandon them, but settled them in Makkah).

10. Daughters of god
and 27 in the New Testament.

11. 66 books (39 in the Old Testament

12. Psalms

13. 17th century

14. Leviticus

15. St. Paul

16. Exodus

Ladies in the Qur'ān

1. Queen Bilqīs, Queen of Sheba

2. Maryam or Mary

3. Sarah

4. Mūsā's mother

5. Fir'awn's wife, Āsiyah

6. Zainab bint Jahsh

7. Maryam

8. Maryam

9. Lūt's wife

10. Aziz's wife, Zulaikhā

11. 'A'ishah

12. Daughters of Lūt (see 11:78)

13. Sarah (see 51:29)

14. Fir'awn's wife, Āsiyah

15. Aziz's wife, Zulaikhā

16. Wives of the Prophet (33:28)

17. Queen Bilqīs, as she entered the palace of Sulaimān (27:44)

The Difference

1. The sūrah does not begin with *Bismillahir Rahmanir Rahim*.

2. It has two directions of Qiblah.

3. It is the first mosque ever built by the Muslims, and it was the first mosque built by the Prophet.

4. *Assalatu Khairun Minan Nawm* (salāt is better than sleep) is mentioned twice in the Adhān.

5. No sujud or prostration is done in the prayer. Also, it is done in standing mode.

6. Fighting is prohibited in the four sacred months

7. She was the only unmarried woman to marry the Prophet. All other wives were widow or divorced by others.

8. They married the Prophet's daughters.

9. The father, Abū Talib did not accept Islam

10. Zainab was married to Abū-l 'Ā s, other daughters were married to Companions who would later become Rightly guided Khalifa.

11. First time a torn, blood tinged shirt was used by brothers to prove that he was dead, the second time they presented a nice shirt to prove he was alive.

12. There was no true battle. The Quraish were devastated by violent storm and they left with a sense of defeat, despair and empty handed.
13. With Saudah the Prophet led a monogamous life as with Khadījah. Later he married other women and led a polygamous marital life.

Before And After

1. 'Umar
2. Maryam
3. 'Isa
4. Killing of an Egyptian
5. Shirt tinged with blood
6. Gold
7. Wahy or revelation (20:38)
8. Saudah
9. The woman referred to was the wife of Ibrāhīm
10. Abdūl Muttalib
11. Khadījah
12. 'Umar Ibn Al-Khattāb
13. Shirt of Yūsuf (12:96)
14. Abū Tālib. His sons Ja'far and 'Ali were Muslims, but not he.
15. Ruqayyah, 'Uthman married her sister Umm Kulthum
16. Lūt, who was nephew of Ibrāhīm

Juz Amma

1. 37 sūrahs
2. Naba'
3. Kauthar
4. Ad-Duhā (93:6-7)
5. Al-Fīl, refers to attack of Abrahah, happened in 570 C.E.
6. Ikhlās
7. Khannas
8. 'Ādiyat
9. Qadr
10. Mā'ūn
11. Al-Qāri'ah
12. Twisted palm coir (111:5)
13. Al-Qāri'ah
14. Al-'Alaq (96:4)
15. At-Tīn (95:1-3)
16. Naba', the word is mentioned in v. 1 of the sūrah

Middle East Conflict

1. Fatah
2. Ramallah
3. Shimon Peres
4. Munich
5. Shatil and Shabra
6. Balfour Declaration
7. Jordan
8. Oslo Accord
9. Egypt
10. Intifada
11. Hamas
12. Mossad
13. Mahmud Abbas
14. Golda Meir
15. Black September

How Many

1. 40 rak'at (4+10+8+5+13)
2. Four times
3. 950 years (29:14)
4. 2 years
5. 3 daughters – Ruqayyah, Umm Kulthum and Fatimah
6. 40 nights
7. 2 years
8. 3 days
9. 3 days (5:89)
10. 4 months, they are Muharram, Rajab, Dhul Qadah and Dhul Hajj
11. 354 days,
12. 10 companions
13. 4-months and 10 days (2:234)
14. Three months (2:228; 65:4)
15. Until deliver of the baby (65:4)
16. 25-years, she died when she was 65 years old
17. 1,000 nights (97:3)

Legal Ruling

1. Halāl
2. Harām
3. Makrūh
4. Swine or Pig
5. Any intoxicating drink, e.g. wine.
6. Kindness to parents
7. Backbiting.
8. Dhul- Hajj
9. Four
10. Two females
11. Husband's
12. Near Ka'bah
13. 'Iddat
14. Adopted children are not entitled to inheritance share
15. Sin
16. Zakat

"Abū-"

1. Abū-Tālib
2. Abū-Bakr
3. Abū-Bakr
4. Abū-Hurairah
5. Abū-Lahab
6. Abū-Sufyān
7. Abū-l- Qāsim, people fondly called him by as the father of Qāsim, the first son of the Prophet.
8. Abū- Bakr
9. Abū- Jahl
10. Abū Ubaidah ibn Al-Jarrah
11. Abū Dhabi
12. Abū Muslim
13. Abū Nidal
14. Abū Dāwūd
15. Zamakhsharī
16. Abū Lahab
17. Abu Al-Qasim (936-1013)

Miscellaneous – I

1. Olive tree
2. Mikā'īl
3. 'Azrā'īl
4. Masjid Al-Aqsa
5. Ezra or 'Uzair
6. A Tower
7. Zaqqūm
8. Zayd
9. Abd Allāh ibn Ubayy
10. Jālūt or Goliath
11. Abd Allāh Ibh Ubayy
12. Abū Lahab
13. Negus of Abyssinia
14. Sarah, wife of Ibrāhīm
15. Zakariyyāh
16. Sabbath
17. Wahshī
18. Sa'd Ibn Mu'adh, a member of Aws, close ally of Banu Qurayzah

Miscellaneous – II

1. Mūsā
2. Sāmirī
3. A dog
4. A day or part of it.
5. 300 years (18:25).
6. Made a hole in the boat
7. Rajab
8. Mosquito or gnat
9. Bakkah
10. Abū Sufyān
11. 'Ad
12. Children of Ādam
13. They have sūrah in their name
14. Harām
15. Female goddesses in pre Islamic Arabia
16. Umm Salmah

Miscellaneous – III

1. Lūt
2. Alif Lām Mīm
3. Sālih
4. Hūd
5. Al- Qāsim, Al-Tahīr
6. Mūsā
7. Ten most distinguished followers of the Prophet, about whom it was said they will enter paradise.
8. Fire, although fire is not an element.
9. Hākim
10. Suhuf
11. Saum
12. Hubal
13. Hāshim
14. Du'ā Qunūt
15. Khawarij
16. Iron (see 18:96)
17. Maysarah

Miscellaneous – IV

1. Battle of Badr
2. Ramadān
3. Balfour Declaration
4. 'Ali Ibn Abī Tālib
5. Tā Hā, Sūrah #20
6. Ramallāh in the West Bank
7. Abū Lahab
8. 1/25th (1/5th share out of 1/5th State share) (see: 8:41)
9. Silk Road
10. His party Hamas won the election
11. Abū Ghraib
12. Shu'aib
13. Shimon Peres and Yitzhak Rabin
14. Lawrence of Arabia
15. Lion of the Desert (1981)

The Last

1. Maimunah
2. 'Ali
3. An-Nasr
4. An-Nās
5. Fātimah
6. Ibrāhīm – born to him from his Coptic wife Mariah
7. The battle of Hunain
8. He repaired a wall that was crumbling down (18:77)
9. Hussain
10. Sun (6:78)
11. 'Abdullāh
12. Imam Hanbal
13. Fātimah, she died 6 months after the Prophet's death. All his children died before his death.
14. 'Ā'ishah
15. An Imam named Muhammad, he disappeared in 878 C.E. Shī'ites believe he would return as Mahdī,
16. Sidratul Muntaha
17. Uhud

How to Conduct In-School Quiz Competition

Islamic quiz competition is a great way to motivate students to learn about Islam, in reasonably short period of time. The schools that routinely organize such competition vouch for it. Unlike organizing inter-school quiz competition, in-school competition is fairly easy to organize. The following ideas may help many weekend or full time schools to organize annual in-school quiz competition.

In an in-school quiz competition each participant will compete at individual level. The idea is to test the competence of each participant rather than of a team. Allow as many participants as possible to compete. However, if far too many contestants show interest, the quiz competition may be split in two levels—an elimination round followed by a final round. Ideal place to hold such a competition is a large room, a gym or even the floor of the mosque, if the school meets inside a mosque.

Prior preparations for the Competition
* Decide whether you want to ask questions topic-wise or simply mix them together. Mixing them together is probably better idea for in-school competitions. Have a good blend of easy, medium and small number of hard questions.
* Decide how long you want to run the competition, then pick total number of questions.
* Ideally 60-70 questions should be a good number to run the competition. This would take about one and half to two hours to conduct and finish the competition.
* Decide whether you want to use overhead projectors or PowerPoint projections.
* If you want to use overhead projectors, conserve the transparency. Print three questions in one transparency and cut the transparency for each question. Have them separated by white paper inserts. If questions are mixed together, all questions can be placed back to back in one stack. If you prefer to ask questions topic-wise, stack them by topics.
* Make sure you invite parents. Involving parents is a great idea to promote learning through their patronage and encouragement.
* Create a budget for the competition. If needed, seek small donations. You may want to reward first three place winners with medals, books or certificates.

Conducting the Quiz Competition:
* Have the contestants sit in a semicircle format rather than in two or three rows.
* The Quiz Master will preferably be at the center of the semicircle.
* The scoring should be done by a different person, preferably an adult.
* Allocate equal points for all questions, e.g. 100.
* Do not deduct points for incorrect answer. Allow the contestants to guess.

- Sitting arrangements of the contestants should be done through draw of lots.
- For each question contestant will get only one chance to answer.
- Ask questions in a clockwise direction, starting from person 'A'. If 'A' gets the first question but cannot answer it, let the question passes on to 'B'. If 'B' cannot answer it will pass on to 'C' and so on until answer is found, but it will not go back to 'A'.
- The first candidate who gets a question should get ten seconds to answer. But all 'pass' questions should be answered immediately by the next contestant. If not answered immediately, it will continue to pass until an answer is found.
- Regardless of who answered the first question, the second question should be asked to 'B'. Regardless of who answered the second question, the third question should be asked to 'C' and so on.
- If the quiz is mixed bag of questions, ask the questions from the stack one after another by placing them on the overhead projector or clicking on PowerPoint slide show.
- If you decided to have the questions based on specific topics, announce the topics when competition begins. Have the contestant pick a topic. Since all questions have equal points, once a topic is chosen by a contestant, ask the top-most question from the respective topic.
- The scorer should be familiar with all the contestants. Name of each contestant should be written down in the same order they are seated. This will help easy scoring. At the end of the competition add the scores to declare the winner.
- If the competition is based on specific topics, preferably have 6 or 7 questions under each topic.
- It is possible to arrange for buzzer to conduct the quiz. Whoever clicks the buzzer gets to answer, but if the answer is wrong, points should be deducted. Use of buzzer system may complicate the show and probably not warranted for in-school settings.

Variations:

- In a competition involving, say 8 contestants, ask the questions in clockwise direction, starting from contestant A to contestant H. When all contestants got to pick their first questions, reverse the order of asking questions, this time starting with contestant H and going counter clockwise to contestant A.
- A few random questions may be made "open" i.e. whoever selects the question everybody gets to answer it by writing it down on a paper. Ask the contestants to write down their name on the paper ahead of time or print the contestant's name beforehand.

How to Conduct Inter-School Quiz Competition

Detailed planning will be needed if you want to conduct an Inter-School Quiz Competition. The organizing school should have a large auditorium or conference room to accommodate the contestants and visitors from other schools. The organizers should arrange for breakfast/lunch/dinner for the contestants and visitors. If it is a regional competition, many of the participants would be traveling 100 miles or more and they are your guests. Inter-School competition can be held at team or individual basis. Preferably one team consisting of three or four contestants from each school should be allowed to participate in the competition.

Prior preparations for the Competition

In addition to those mentioned under In-School Quiz Competition, planning for Inter-School Quiz Competition will require *four* to *five months* of preparation. This prepraration will be based on the number of participating teams.

- Prepare a budget for the Inter-School Quiz Competition and have it funded.
- Send notifications to all neighboring schools about the upcoming competition. Mention date, place and time. Invite them to participate. Follow up with emails and phone calls.
- Let them know the format of the quiz so that they may prepare accordingly. If possible send them one page sample questions and recommend this quiz book or other books and the Internet to facilitate preparation.
- Follow up with the principals of the schools and obtain confirmations from participating schools.
- Arrange for microphones, one for the Quiz Master and one for the contestants. Since arranging separate microphones for each team is a costly affair, have someone physically carry a cordless or corded microphone to each team.
- Preferably use PowerPoint projections to display each question.
- As some teams may have travelled long distance, provide snacks before the competition, and a simple meal after. Form a sub-committee to arrange and oversee the snacks and meals.

Conducting the Quiz Competition:

- Overall guidelines for in-school competition should be followed.
- Contestants of each school will sit together in small clusters, but teams will sit in a semicircle format.
- If large number of schools participate, an elimination round may be held. In order to give the chance to each participants, the elimination round should be elaborate. Top 5 or 6 teams from the elimination round will compete in the final round to decide the final winner. Timing and number of questions to be asked in both the rounds should be carefully calculated in order to finish entire competition in a timely manner.

Bibliography

Ali, Abdullah Yusuf, The Meaning of The Holy Qur'an, 10th ed. (Beltsville: Amana Publications, 1999).

Armstrong, Karen, Islam A Short History (New York: The Modern Library, 2000).

Asad, Muhammad, The Message of the Qur'an (Gibraltar: Dar Al-Andalus, 1980).

Elmasry, Mohamed I., 1000 Questions on Islam (New York: IBTS, 1997).

Emerick, Yahya, What Islam is all About (New York: IBTS, 2000).

Farah, Caesar E., Islam Belief and Observances (New York: Barrons, 2000)

Hoque, Zohurul, Translation and Commentary on The Holy Qur-an (Dayton: Holy Qur-an Publishing Project, 2000).

Hughes, Thomas Patrick, Dictionary of Islam (Chicago: Kazi Publications, 1994).

Lings, Martin, Muhammad: His Life Based on the Earliest Stories (London: Foundation for Traditional Studies, 1983).

Lunde, Peter, Islam (New York: DK Publishing, Inc. 2002).

Rahman, Fazlur, Islam (Chicago: University of Chicago Press, 1979).

Robinson, Neal, Islam A Concise Introduction (Washington DC: Georgetown University Press, 1999).

Siddiqui, Jamal-un-Nisa, IQ Islamic Quiz Book (1) & (2) (London: Ta-Ha Publishers Ltd., 1997).

The 1999 Grolier Multimedia Encyclopedia One Disc Edition, Ver. 11.00 (Grolier Interactive, Inc, 1998).

Thomson, Ahmad, The Wives of the Prophet Muhammad (London: Ta-Ha Publishers Ltd., 1993).

Zepp, Ira G., Jr. A Muslim Primer Beginners Guide to Islam (Fayetteville: University of Arkansas Press, 2000).

Encyclopaedia Britannica 2001 Standard Edition, CD-ROM

Notes

Notes